DIFFERENTIATION FOR GIFTED STUDENTS
IN A SECONDARY SCHOOL

DIFFERENTIATION FOR GIFTED STUDENTS
IN A SECONDARY SCHOOL

A HANDBOOK FOR TEACHERS
EDITED BY DR SUSAN NIKAKIS

Copyright © 2022 selection and editorial matter, Susan Nikakis; individual chapters, the contributors

All rights reserved. No part of this book may be reproduced or transmitted in any form or by any means, electronic or mechanical, including photocopying, recording or by any information storage and retrieval system, without prior permission in writing from the publisher.

Published by Amba Press
Melbourne, Australia
www.ambapress.com.au

Cover designer – Tess McCabe

ISBN: 9781922607409 (pbk)
ISBN: 9781922607416 (ebk)

A catalogue record for this book is available from the National Library of Australia.

CONTENTS

Acknowledgements	vii
About the editor	viii
About the contributors	ix
Introduction by Susan Nikakis	1

1. Who are these gifted students?   11
   Susan Nikakis

2. Models of differentiation and how to use them   33
   Susan Nikakis

3. What else is available for gifted secondary students?   59
   Mark Smith

4. Re/engaging and developing creatively gifted thinkers in mixed ability classrooms   74
   Amy Horneman

5. Providing school transitions for gifted and talented students   97
   Carmel Meehan

6. Programs and programming in secondary schools   114
   Geraldine Nicholas

7. Curriculum differentiation for gifted students in secondary science classes   131
   Christine Ireland

8. Differentiating learning with STEM education inquiry projects Part 1 – Theory   144
   Shelley Waldon

9. Differentiating learning with STEM education inquiry projects Part 2 – Practice   160
   Shelley Waldon

10. Attending to the needs of the emotionally gifted student   182
    Arrigo Dorissa

11. Student voice and comments from students   194
    Susan Nikakis

ACKNOWLEDGEMENTS

I would like to express my eternal gratitude to my fellow authors for sharing their expertise and experience. All are friends as well as colleagues. Their dedication to assisting gifted students reach their potential is truly inspirational.

I met our publisher Alicia at an education summit. Serendipity or fate made this book a reality under her skilled guidance.

ABOUT THE EDITOR

Dr Susan Nikakis is an educator in the gifted arena and an executive member of the Victorian Association for Gifted and Talented Children (VAGTC). She has taught in six secondary schools as well as lectured at the university level. She has been instrumental in editing three books related to gifted education. Susan has presented papers centred on the education of gifted students in many countries around the world. Her drive to finish this compilation was not diminished by the COVID-19 pandemic.

ABOUT THE CONTRIBUTORS

Arrigo Dorissa

Arrigo Dorissa is a psychologist and writer. Most of his professional career has focused on educational settings. His most rewarding efforts are in assisting school communities with cultivating learning environments in which the cognitive and creative potential of all students, not just the gifted, can be maximised. He lives in a city that he loves; Melbourne, also known as Naarm, on the unceded land of the Wurundjeri and Boon Wurrung peoples of the Kulin nation.

Amy Horneman

Amy Horneman started her career in education as a secondary English and German teacher, and through years of gathering experience teaching across many subject areas and from prep through to year 12, has ended up delving deeply into the field of gifted and talented education. She is passionate about mentoring gifted and highly-able students through their schooling years; developing students in leadership; collaborating with key stakeholders to implement schoolwide provisions for gifted and highly-able students; and fostering positive and effective home-school partnerships. She is currently the coordinator of the gifted education program at Scotch College in Melbourne, and is an active committee member (consultant, seminar writer and presenter, and magazine editor) of the Victorian Association for Gifted and Talented Children (VAGTC). She holds a Bachelor of Arts/Education (Secondary) and Master of Arts (Applied Linguistics), and has completed postgraduate studies in educational leadership and gifted education.

Christine Ireland
Christine Ireland is an ex-president of the Victorian and Australian Associations for Gifted Education. She lectured in Victorian universities, co-ordinated primary and secondary schools' gifted education, is completing a doctorate of gifted education and has presented over twenty national and international papers in gifted education events, books and magazines. Christine has co-ordinated gifted education programs in primary and secondary schools, and has taught English, science, history and geography for over 20 years.

Carmel Meehan
Carmel Meehan is a life member of the Victorian Association for Gifted and Talented Children Inc. joining in 2003. She publishes articles in magazines/books, speaks about giftedness on radio and television, delivers papers and seminars nationally and internationally including at four World Council Conferences and the Dabrowski Congress. Employment included principal of four Catholic primary schools; education consultant; scaffolding school principals in the areas of leadership development, curriculum performance, gifted and talented educational programmes and whole of school review. Carmel holds TITC, B. Ed, Grad Dip of Ed (Religious Education), Basic Counselling Skills Certificate, Master of Education, Post Graduate Certificate of Education (Gifted Education).

Geraldine Nicholas
Geraldine Nicholas is the professional learning coordinator for Tournament of Minds. This program has been around for 35 years and continues to enchant and enthral students across all sectors and year levels. Geraldine has also worked in several schools across both primary and secondary years as gifted coordinator teaching within the gifted program. She has experience in developing and reviewing gifted programs. Geraldine has worked with schools across Victoria over many years to develop inquisitive students who can thrive in a creative environment. She has an ongoing commitment to meeting the needs of gifted and talented students.

Mark Smith
Mark Smith is an innovative educator with more than 25 years' experience in the Victorian independent school system. He holds a Master of Education, Gifted and Talented Education acquired via course work and research at Monash University. Mark is best known for his work in gifted and talented education where he has created and implemented large multi-faceted school wide programs at some of Melbourne's largest independent schools. He is passionate about guided inquiry-based learning approaches and has facilitated outstanding results with students of all ages using mentoring as a means of cultivating questioning skills, and deep, engaging personal research processes, to foster student connection and autonomy. His students have had outstanding successes and won many academic awards and tertiary scholarships in a wide range of academic fields.

Shelley Waldon
Shelley Waldon has experience working with industry, government, cultural and educational organisations. As a Melbourne Archdiocese Catholic Schools (MACS) school representative on steering committees for cross-sectoral STEM-education, Shelley is recognised as a leader in the field of STEM education and an enabler, advancing STEM education in Catholic schools utilising the trusting relationship she has established with teachers and schools. In her present role as the MACS Science & STEM Lead, Shelley Waldon leads STEM conferences, student showcases, workshops and professional learning for Catholic schools.

INTRODUCTION

SUSAN NIKAKIS

*If you don't know where you are going,
you might wind up someplace else.*
– Yogi Berra

WHY WRITE THIS BOOK?

What was the motivation in editing and compiling this book? As a secondary teacher initially and now an educational consultant in gifted education I was frustrated that I had to use so many different resources to assist secondary teachers differentiate the curriculum. With a plethora of gifted teachers contributing chapters taken directly from their own life experience. I encourage you to discover new ideas for your students and indeed some of your teachers.

Why ask a group of experts in this area to write about various aspects of differentiation for gifted secondary students? Surely secondary school teachers learnt about teaching those higher achieving students at university? One would presume that these teachers had been taught to differentiate their unique curriculum in order to engage all learners? It is a disturbing fact that few universities in Australia offer courses in teaching gifted students let alone gifted secondary students! All of the authors in this collection have been or are members of their state, national or international gifted associations. They are all volunteers in their associations dedicated to improving the educational life of gifted students.

In my 35 years as a secondary teacher in Melbourne Australia, I did indeed learn about catering for the needs of gifted students from some highly skilled teachers. The vast majority of secondary school trained teachers I taught alongside were certainly experts in their areas of expertise. The history teachers could bring alive the gold rushes in Victoria. As a student in past decades learning in one of these classes I loved learning about the excitement of discovery and the many social and emotional hardships which accompanied work on the goldfields. When it came to demonstrating my knowledge about what I had learnt however, there was only one way with no choice. Comprehension questions or perhaps an essay but certainly no choice in assessment task and every student was supposed to answer the identical essay question. Was there choice for the very creative students in the class? No. Were there less complex tasks for the students who found learning history challenging? No. Were there different formats in which the information could be presented? No. Was that lack of choice boring? Yes!

So how do we make learning interesting and stimulating without exhausting the teacher?

Teachers strive to instil a love of learning in their students. But many find it difficult to work effectively with gifted children, whose educational needs fall outside the norm. The depth, intensity and exceptional thirst for learning among gifted students place unexpected demands on teachers, often ill-equipped to manage these children's needs. With little training in giftedness, lack of administrative support, and competing demands in a heterogeneous learning environment, many teachers face an uphill battle.

Some secondary teachers will be at the beginning of their learning journey about differentiating the curriculum for gifted students, some teachers will want a refresher and some, if not all, hope that they can find an idea easily!

Teaching is a tough job, especially when schools face a lack of funding and resources. Teachers' jobs are frequently undervalued, scapegoated and under attack. If you want to make your job more manageable, and certainly if you want to excel in your work with gifted children, finding the support you need is critical.

Enlist the support of others (teachers, parents, administration, school boards, and advocates, state gifted organisations) to insist that the schools set up classroom structures and universal pre-screening so that gifted children receive the fair and appropriate education they deserve. Pay attention to any false assumptions you might harbor about gifted children, and get as educated as possible about their needs.

The short-term goal is to find a template or a novel approach to use for differentiation of the curriculum. The long-term goal might be to use the book as a professional learning enrichment tool or a guide on the side.

Much has been written about Australia's dismal performance with our brightest students as reflected in OECD PISA data (2021). We are as a nation coping with the needs of our struggling students on the left side of the bell curve. We are not catering well for our students on the right side of the bell curve. Our most gifted students just cruise through school 'doing' the least amount of work and still succeeding (according to the norms in the classroom). This does not even take into account those truly gifted underachievers. Our goal in this book is to have teachers focussing on these adolescent years and all the challenges that brings with gifted students.

For the purposes of this book these basic definitions give us a base on which to build knowledge.

A differentiated curriculum is a learning program that, ideally, meets the academic needs and interests of every student. This means that all teaching approaches outlined in the curriculum are flexible, so that the content being taught is digestible and refreshingly challenging for each individual student. You can also differentiate the way you present the information or the process, differentiate the presentation modes or indeed change the environment within the classroom. This is the basis of the book and there will be examples throughout.

I have found that if you teach your students how the differentiation works then at times they can even write the differentiated questions! This is actually marvellous teaching and learning as your students understand the differences in levels and complexity.

The definition of being gifted, is to have above-average intelligence and/or superior talent for something such as music, art, or math. Many school-based programs for the gifted select children who have superior intellectual skills and academic aptitude. However, children can be gifted in other areas such as the arts, sport and leadership. The lack of a stable definition will always be a quandary when looking at how to educate the gifted. However, what is important to educators who are practising in the field, are the characteristics they display. Worrell et al. define being gifted as exhibiting superior performance in a domain to their peers (Worrell et al., 2019). The definition of *giftedness* in terms of high intelligence has been extended and now includes the concepts of 'creativity' and 'talent'. Definitions, however, are diverse – some compete with each other, and all depend on what is valued in a culture.

COMMON CHARACTERISTICS OF GIFTED CHILDREN

While no two gifted children are the same, research has shown that most gifted learners exhibit many common characteristics and behaviours. The following are common characteristics of gifted children, although not all will necessarily apply to every gifted child:
- Has an extensive and detailed memory particularly in a specific area of interest
- Has advanced vocabulary for their age; uses precocious language
- Has communication skills advanced for their age and is able to express ideas and feelings

- Asks intelligent and complex questions
- Is able to identify the important characteristics of new concepts and problems
- Learns information quickly
- Uses logic in arriving at common sense answers
- Has a broad base of knowledge
- Understands abstract ideas and complex concepts
- Uses analogical thinking problem solving or reasoning
- Observes relationships and sees connections
- Finds and solves difficult and unusual problems
- Understands principles, forms generalisations and uses them in new situations
- Wants to learn and is curious
- Works conscientiously and has a high degree of concentration in areas of interest
- Understands and uses various symbol systems
- Is reflective about learning
- Is enraptured by a specific subject
- Has reading comprehension skills advanced for their age
- Has advanced writing abilities for their age
- Has strong artistic or musical abilities
- Concentrates intensely for long periods of time particularly in a specific area of interest
- Is more aware; stimulated and affected by surroundings
- Experiences extreme positive or negative feelings
- Experiences a strong physical reaction to emotion
- Has a strong affective memory reliving or refeeling things long after the triggering event.

SO, WHAT'S IN IT FOR YOU?

Chapter one is all about necessary definitions of giftedness. A brief history and models of giftedness can be very informative and you can share it with your teaching staff. The importance of identifying students cannot be emphasised too much. The exploration of the diversity of gifted students is a highlight of this chapter. You can use much of this information to inform your own understanding and the understanding of your colleagues.

Chapter two is about curriculum differentiation where models are explored. This chapter contains theory, practice and examples which may offer ideas which you can work with in your classroom. There are also many strategies to inform your teaching and share with others. This is a user friendly and useful introductory chapter for secondary teachers. This chapter will be very useful for novice teachers and hopefully will be very instructive. I find when I attend professional learning on differentiation that presenters stick to theory when teachers really want practical examples they can use in the classroom tomorrow! This is a pivotal chapter in the book. Myths about gifted students and differentiation are also included. The references are useful for teachers who want to peruse any area.

Chapter three covers programs which work in schools. There are some great ideas for you to use in the classroom. Mark Smith has rich and varied experiences in secondary gifted programs and he shares a year 9 program outline which can be really useful experience to teachers looking for ideas for their gifted students. Mark writes about a range of competitions and programs. He also talks about Kanevsky's (2017) possibilities for learning which is very instructive and can broaden your knowledge base in relation to catering for the needs of gifted students. I am a big fan of the Tournament of Minds competition and Mark explains how to use it to stimulate your gifted students. Student voice is very important and this too is explored in this chapter. Links to various websites are an important facet of this chapter. The case studies are really useful for teachers to discuss at staff meetings.

Chapter four delves into re/engaging and developing creatively gifted thinkers in mixed ability classrooms. Here you will meet student Vlad who you will all recognise from your own classroom. There are wonderful illustrations and you will further your knowledge of Françoys Gagné's work on differentiation. His developmental model of giftedness and talent 2 (DMGT 2.0) is a widely accepted and utilised model for talent development across Australia.

Author Amy unpacks the Maker model of differentiated curriculum which is very user friendly for teachers new to teaching gifted students. The Learning Pit is also explored in relation to differentiating for secondary gifted students. Original student artwork is a feature of this chapter. Mihaly Csikszentmihalyi is looked to as one of the most eminent experts on creativity worldwide, and his theory of 'flow'; is described with clarity by Amy.

Chapter five is a chapter about how well your school provides for the transition of gifted and talented students. You can't differentiate for a gifted year 7 student if they arrive at secondary school with no transition information to inform teachers. Author Carmel talks about the all important aspect of the social and emotional wellbeing of our gifted secondary students. Linda Silverman's (2002) characteristics of gifted students work is highlighted in this chapter and can only add to the body of knowledge this book provides.

Asynchronous development relates to the development of students who have a high ability in some academic areas but may not have a similar ability level in all curriculum areas. This chapter also addresses the issues of bullying, dumbing down and concludes with a really useful 'Transition Awareness's Audit for Reflection and Discussion' section. Another interesting aspect of this chapter is Carmel's section on spiritual giftedness.

Chapter six covers the all important area of identification of gifted students. Author Geraldine uses the Rogers (2017) learning profiles scale and mentions specific tests which can be used by teachers. Delivery options are explored and cluster grouping and pull out programs are examined as options for catering for the needs of gifted secondary students. Renzulli's school enrichment model (SEM) is a great way to differentiate for gifted secondary students. Twice exceptional (2e) students who are gifted coupled with a disability are explained. Geraldine also writes about tests which are available to identify and diagnose gifted secondary students. Selective schools are discussed.

Chapter seven is specifically related to curriculum differentiation for gifted students in secondary science classes. Christine writes about gifted underachievement and the reasons differentiation of the curriculum is so vital for gifted secondary students. She uses science as a key learning area to demonstrate differentiation techniques. Extension, enrichment and creative problem solving opportunities are explored. A fascinating aspect encompasses what extension and enrichment look like in a science classroom. Christine has just fished her doctoral thesis in this area and I would like to take this opportunity to congratulate her on her ground-breaking work.

Chapter eight is entitled differentiating learning for secondary students with STEM education inquiry projects and Part 1 looks at the theory (the what and why of STEM education) and is full of exciting ideas and case studies. Author Shelley's focus on fertile questions as described by includes their list of rich characteristics. Even non-STEM teachers will learn much from this informative chapter about catering for the needs of gifted secondary students and leads beautifully into chapter nine.

Chapter nine is a continuation of chapter eight and author, Shelley, looks at the more practical side of designing stimulating learning experiences for gifted students. She shares how a differentiated science education can offer:
- a strong vision for integrated education that is underpinned by deep knowledge, understanding of research and system directions and a recognition of context
- teachers as designers of learning who promote collaboration and problem solving as essential learning capabilities for themselves and their students and ensure equitable access and opportunity for all.

The provocations, contentious issues and initiating questions section is a real hook for teachers. Project based learning is an important aspect of this chapter and teachers will indeed be enlightened. The STEM designed inquiry projects will be a great guide for teachers. The STEM visual will be a saviour for most teachers in this area and is very impressive.

Chapter ten is written by an educational psychologist and includes a fascinating case study of a gifted secondary student. Arrigo includes a framework for a more inclusive learning environment. The social and emotional wellbeing of gifted and talented students continues to be recognised as an educational psychology matter and not within mainstream educational practices. For advocates of gifted and talented students these matters remain of significant importance. Gifted students often continue to be academically and creatively under challenged at secondary schools and some remain in danger of developing mental health issues. An informative list of factors for the engagement with learning is important for all teachers of gifted secondary students. A wider lens that considers social and emotional needs of gifted learners is a proposal that is of timely importance.

Chapter eleven contains direct quotes and reflections directly from gifted secondary students. Student voice is very important when planning for all learning especially those of our gifted students. One way to provide students with a voice is by giving them a platform to express themselves. This can come in multiple forms. You can set up a morning meeting at homeroom where students have the opportunity to discuss things they are feeling or events either inside or outside of school. This of course needs tight parameters with secondary students so guidelines for these discussions need to be negotiated with the student. Some students need to be in a smaller group because they have more difficulty maintaining all the social relationships in a discussion, whereas others are more skilled at doing so and can be in larger groups. This is particularly important to twice exceptional (2e) gifted students and gifted students who suffer from anxiety. You can also use an old fashioned anonymous questions box.

Ideally, our classrooms would be places where students not only gain knowledge but also discover who they are and who they want to be. Prioritising student voice strengthens a sense of belonging, as the learning experiences are co-created by students and teachers.

Elevating student voice is critical for many reasons. For one thing, as Douglas Fisher and Nancy Frey (2014) write, "The amount of talk that students do is correlated with their achievement."

As John Hattie (2012) reminds us, "A positive, caring, respectful climate in the classroom is a prior condition to learning." Strong teacher-student relationships bolster students' confidence to share their voices.

There are many models which cover curriculum delivery appropriate for secondary students. Many of these will be covered in the ensuing chapters. The mantra for all gifted students should be 'different not more'. We hope you enjoy and learn more about catering for your gifted secondary students.

CHAPTER REFERENCES

Betts, G. and Neihart, M. (2015). Profiles of the Gifted and Talented. Davidson Institute for Talent Development. Reprinted from *Gifted Child Quarterly*, National Association for Gifted Children (NAGC) 1988. Web. July 2015

Fisher, D and Frey, N. (2014). *Formative Assessment Techniques for Your Classroom.*

Gagné, F. (2010). Transforming gifts into talents: the DMGT as a developmental theory, *High Ability Studies*, 15:2, 119–147

Gardner, H.E. (2000). *Intelligence reframed: Multiple intelligences for the 21st century*. Hachette UK

Harpaz, Y. and Lefstein, A. (2000). Communities of Thinking. *Educational Leadership*, v58 n3 p54–57

Hattie, J. (2012). *Visible Learning for Teachers: Maximizing Impact on Learning*, Routledge

Kanevsky L. (2013). *The Tool Kit for High End Curriculum Differentiation*. Burnaby, Can.: Simon Fraser University

OECD (2021) Education at a glance 2021: OECD indicators, OECD publishing, Paris

Renzulli, J. (1997). How to develop an authentic enrichment cluster, National Research Centre on the Gifted and Talented, ERIC Document reproduction service no. ED 420594

Rogers, K. (2017). 'Academic effects research synthesis', in S Assouline, N Colangelo, J VanTassel-Baska & A Lupkowski-Shoplik (eds), A nation empowered: Evidence trumps the excuses holding back America's brightest students, *The Connie Belin & Jacqueline N. Blank International Centre for Gifted Education and Talent Development*, Iowa City, IA, pp. 19–30

Ronksley-Pavia, M. (2020). Personalised learning: Disability and gifted learners. In *Teaching Primary Years: Rethinking Curriculum, Pedagogy, and Assessment;* Pendergast, D., Main, K., Eds.; Allen & Unwin: Crows Nest, Australia, 2019; pp. 422–442

Worrell, F. C., Subotnik, R. F., Olszewski-Kubilius, P., & Dixson, D. D. (2019). Gifted students. *Annual Review of Psychology*, 70, 551–576. https://doi.org/10.1146/annurev-psych-010418-102846

CHAPTER I

WHO ARE THESE GIFTED STUDENTS?

SUSAN NIKAKIS

The biggest mistake of past centuries in teaching has been to treat all students as if they were variants of the same individual and thus to feel justified in teaching them all the same subjects the same way.
– Howard Gardner

In 2027, giftedness was defined as the potential for superior achievement in an area that is valuable for the society, (Davis et al., 2017), but the definition is continuously evolving.

This chapter will give you some background in the following areas:
- Giftedness – The beginning
- Who are these gifted students?

- How to identify gifted students
- Social and emotional giftedness
- Models and theories of giftedness.

GIFTEDNESS – THE BEGINNING

Supposedly, the field of gifted education is almost 150 years old, dating from Galton's (1869) publication of *Hereditary Genius*. Others think that giftedness was quite apparent in the time of Socrates and Plato and Australia's first peoples have demonstrated giftedness in many areas for 60,000 years. Giftedness has been sought after and valued throughout the ages. Giftedness is a dynamic concept which reflects changes in societies' needs and priorities, therefore, some discrepancy is inevitable.

Gifted and talented students are entitled to rigorous, relevant and engaging learning opportunities drawn from the Australian Curriculum (or their own country's curriculum). These students need their curriculum to be aligned with their individual learning needs, strengths, interests and goals. Gifted students are those who exhibit superior performance in a particular domain relative to peers. Nonetheless the discourse on gifted students in Australia can be contradictory and fractious. In this chapter, definitions and models of giftedness will be explored.

Gifted children come from all walks of life. Sometimes people use the terms, *high ability* or *highly able* to describe gifted students. The term *high ability* can sometimes be used in place of the term *gifted*. According to Françoys Gagné (2010), being gifted and being talented are not the same thing. Many teachers, researchers and educators around the world use the term *high ability* but the term *gifted* is more widely used. Gagné differentiates clearly between gifts which are natural abilities, and talents which are systematically developed from gifts. Gagné thinks that all talents are developed from natural abilities through learning, and are influenced by inner and outer catalysts such as personal traits and environmental influences. In Australia, Gagné's differentiated model of giftedness and talent 2.0 is adopted in most contexts related to the education and support of gifted and talented children and youth; this includes organisations such as the Victorian Association of Gifted and Talented (VAGTC) and the Victorian Department of Education. We will elaborate Gagné's model later in the chapter.

Australia is well-known for supporting the 'underdog' and 'keeping tall poppies in check'. Some people think that if someone is labelled as *gifted*, that means they are better than other people. So there is a reluctance to use the label. This is seen in other countries too. But some countries are more accepting than others. For example, in many states in America, teachers need specialist training and accreditation to work with gifted students in their schools. We do not have such a requirement for teachers in Australia.

While the Australian teacher education system does not require all pre-service teachers to be specifically trained in working with gifted and high ability students, all schools have a mandate to cater for the learning needs of each student in each class. This means that teachers should be given ongoing training and support by their schools in how to identify what giftedness looks like in the learning behaviours and outcomes of their students. So let's get on with definitions!

WHO ARE THESE GIFTED STUDENTS?

This chapter will give you some background in the following areas:
- **Academic:** This used to be the only area which people thought the word gifted covered. It applies to specific areas of academic learning like reading, mathematics, science, and history.
- **Creative and artistic:** This applies to children who demonstrate advanced skills in visual or performing arts, painting, drawing, sculpting, drama, and dancing.
- **Leadership:** This is evident in areas where children can take the lead in games, group work or classroom organisation.
- **Sport:** This area is probably the most obvious display of giftedness, with success in sport and other physical activities being easy to recognise by all. Running, jumping, and swimming are examples.

Barbara Clarke (2008) divides gifted students into four broad areas; Cognitive, Creative, Affective and Behavioural.

Cognitive	Creative	Affective	Behavioural
Keen power of abstraction	Creativeness and inventiveness	Unusual emotional depth and intensity	Spontaneity
Interest in problem-solving and applying concepts	Keen sense of humour	Sensitivity or empathy to the feelings of others	Boundless enthusiasm
Voracious and early reader	Ability for fantasy	High expectations of self and others, often leading to feelings of frustration	Intensely focused on passions – resists changing activities when engrossed in own interests
Large vocabulary	Openness to stimuli, wide interests	Heightened self-awareness, accompanied by feelings of being different	Highly energetic – needs little sleep or down time
Intellectual curiosity	Intuitiveness	Easily wounded, need for emotional support	Constantly questions
Power of critical thinking, scepticism, self-criticism	Flexibility	Need for consistency between abstract values and personal actions	Insatiable curiosity
Persistent, goal-directed behaviour	Independence in attitude and social behaviour	Advanced levels of moral judgement	Impulsive, eager and spirited
Independence in work and study	Self-acceptance and unconcern for social norms	Idealism and sense of justice	Perseverance – strong determination in areas of importance
Diversity of interests and abilities	Radicalism		High levels of frustration – particularly when having difficulty meeting standards of performance (either imposed by self or others)
	Aesthetic and moral commitment to self-selected work		Volatile temper, especially related to perceptions of failure
			Non-stop talking, chattering

Figure 1: The four board catagories of gifted students
Source: Clark, B. 2008.

Giftedness comes in many forms. There are many traits that gifted individuals have in common, but no gifted learner exhibits traits in every area. Here is an identification checklist to consider.

Traditional characteristics	Characteristics of culturally/ linguistically diverse gifted students	Characteristics of low socio-economic gifted students	Characteristics of gifted students with disabilities
Ability to learn basic skills quickly and easily and retain information with less repetition	May require more repetition or hands-on experiences at an introductory level	Lack of opportunities and access to school-readiness materials may delay acquisition of basic skills	Often struggles to learn basic skills due to cognitive processing difficulties; Needs to learn compensatory strategies in order to acquire basic skills and information
High verbal ability	May have high verbal ability in native language; May rapidly acquire English language skills if they possess academic skills in their home language	Lack of opportunities may delay the development of verbal skills	High verbal ability but extreme difficulty in written language area; May use language in inappropriate ways and at inappropriate times
Early reading ability	May demonstrate strong storytelling ability and ability to read environmental print in home language	Lack of access to reading materials may delay acquisition of reading skills	Frequently has reading problems due to cognitive processing deficits
Keen power of observation	May display high levels of visual memory or auditory memory skills	Strong 'street smarts' – observational skills	Strong observation skills but often has deficits in memory skills
Strong critical thinking, problem-solving and decision-making skills	Strong critical thinking in primary language; often solves problems in creative ways Particularly interested in solving 'real-world' problems	Excels in brainstorming and solving 'real-world' problems; strong critical thinking ability Rapid decision-making skills	Excels in solving 'real-world' problems; outstanding critical thinking and decision-making skills; Can independently develop compensatory skills

Long attention span; Persistent, intense concentration	Long attention span; Persistent, intense concentration	Persistent in areas of interest usually unrelated to school	Frequently has attention deficit problems but may concentrate for long periods in areas of interest
Questioning attitude	Some culturally diverse children are raised not to question authority	Questioning attitude which may at times be demonstrated in a confronting or challenging way	Strong questioning attitude; May appear disrespectful when questioning information, facts (etc.), presented by a teacher
Creative in the generation of thoughts, ideas, actions; innovative	Often displays richness of imagery in ideas, art, music, primary language, etc.; Can improvise with commonplace objects	Strong creative abilities	Unusual imagination; frequently generates original and at times rather 'bizarre' ideas
Takes risks	Degree of risk taking may depend upon the familiarity of the situation based on different cultural experiences	Takes risks often without consideration of consequences	Often unwilling to take risks with regard to academics; takes risks in non-school areas without consideration of consequences
Unusual, often highly developed sense of humour	Humour may be displayed through unique use of language and responses	May use humour to become 'class clown,' to deal with stressful situations, and to avoid trouble	Humour may be used to divert attention from school failure; May use humour to make fun of peers or to avoid trouble
May mature at different rates than age-peers	Accepts responsibilities in the home normally reserved for older children	Often mature earlier than age peers since they must accept responsibilities in the home which are normally reserved for older children or even adults; inexperience may make them appear socially immature	Sometimes appears immature since they may use anger, crying, withdrawal, etc. to express feelings and to deal with difficulties

Strong sense of independence	May be culturally socialised to work in groups rather than independently	Circumstances often have forced the student to become extremely independent and self-sufficient	Requires frequent teacher support and feedback in deficit areas; Highly independent in other areas; often appears to be extremely stubborn and inflexible
Sensitive	May be sensitive particularly to racial or cultural issues	May be critical of self and others including teachers; can understand and express concern about the feelings of others even while engaging in anti-social behaviour	Sensitive regarding disability area(s); highly critical of self and others including teachers; Can express concern about the feelings of others even while engaging in anti-social behaviour
May not be accepted by other children and may feel isolated	May be perceived as a loner due to racial/cultural isolation and/or inability to speak English; entertains self easily using imagination in games and ingenious play	Economic circumstances as well as their giftedness may isolate the student from more financially secure peers	May be perceived as a loner since they do not fit typical model for either a gifted or a learning disabled student; Sometimes has difficulty being accepted by peers due to poor social skills
Exhibits leadership ability	May be a leader in the community but not in the school setting; Demonstrates 'street-wise' behaviour	May be a leader among the more non-traditional students; Demonstrates strong 'street-wise' behaviour; Often excels in brainstorming and problem solving around social issues	Often leaders among the more non-traditional students; demonstrate strong behaviour; The disability may interfere with ability to exercise leadership skills
Wide range of interests	Interests may include individual culturally related activities	Wide range of interests that are often unrelated to topics/subjects addressed in school	Wide range of interests but is handicapped in pursuing them due to process/learning problems

Differentiation for gifted students

Very focused interests, i.e., a passion about a certain topic to the exclusion of others	Very focused interests, i.e., a passion about a certain topic to the exclusion of others	Very focused interests, i.e., a passion about a certain topic to the exclusion of others – usually not related to school subjects	Very focused interests, i.e., a passion about a certain topic to the exclusion of others – usually not related to school subjects

Figure 2: Identification checklist
Source: Vision Magazine, Supplementary Issue: Checklists (c)

SOCIAL AND EMOTIONAL GIFTEDNESS

This area is often overlooked by secondary school teachers.

Occasionally, students' gifts are not recognised because they think 'outside the box'. Teachers must develop an awareness of the existence of these students and an understanding of their intellectual and social-emotional needs. The social and emotional aspects of giftedness are also crucial to understanding the learning needs of gifted children.

Because gifted teenagers demonstrate greater maturity in some domains over others, they may be at greater risk for specific kinds of social-emotional difficulties if their needs are not met.

These aspects may include heightened awareness, anxiety, perfectionism, stress, issues with peer relationships, and concerns with identity and fit.

At the risk of looking like a chapter of lists, the social and emotional traits of gifted students include:

- Different interests and hobbies to peers. These students can have hobbies that are very adult based.
- An inborn sensitivity is related to existential questioning and an acute awareness of life. Sometimes this can be under the 'emotional excitabilities' banner (see Dabrowski's 1996 work).
- A heightened sense of empathy and compassion. At times this student finds life a struggle and often takes on the problems of the world.
- A strong sense of justice and fairness which can lead to risks to their interpersonal relationships. They often advocate for the 'underdog.'

- A mature sense of humour. These are the students who laugh at a teacher's faux pas.
- Being drawn to older companions or adults. These students are often seen interacting with older students and teachers.
- At an early age, gifted children have to decide whether they will fit in and be accepted or stand out and be rejected – in adolescent years this can also be a serious challenge for gifted students. This is often called forced choice dilemma (Jung, 2011).
- A strong sense of positive self-esteem is critical to the achievement of gifted students. Teachers and others can misunderstand self-esteem, confusing it with conceit rather than a healthy pride in one's abilities.

Keep in mind:
- A student gifted in one area is not necessarily gifted in all areas
- Giftedness can lead to the masking and misunderstanding of problem signs
- Not all gifted students are alike. This includes their unique social-emotional profile
- There is no single, definitive recipe for maintaining a student's emotional equilibrium.

HOW ARE GIFTED STUDENTS VIEWED IN AUSTRALIA?

Gifted students are those who exhibit superior performance in a particular domain relative to peers, however the discourse on gifted students in Australia can be contradictory and fractious. On the one hand, Australians celebrate innovation, creativity and 'out of the box' thinking, but on the other hand, very few educational dollars at either the state or federal level are spent on the education of gifted students. Occasionally, a flurry of funds is injected into our state government schools but this too is a drop in the ocean compared to the ongoing funding for students on the left side of the bell curve or the students with intellectual difficulties or other disabilities.

Students have always come to the classroom varying in socioeconomic status, interests and abilities. The traditional purposes of schooling in a democracy have been to socialise the young, to teach various forms of knowledge which will bring about a realistic and rational view of the world, and to prepare citizens for participation in the democratic way of life. These purposes reflected the nineteenth and twentieth century society (Renzulli, 2001). We are now however in the 21st century and cannot ignore the need for appropriate educational opportunities for all students, especially gifted secondary students.

Although research strongly supports accelerated programming for gifted students (Assouline et al., 2015, Steenbergen-Hu et al., 2016), even support for acceleration is not universal.

Perhaps the most common conceptualisation of giftedness is as high cognitive ability or IQ, a variable that continues to play a major role in most models of giftedness. However, several contemporary conceptualisations extend giftedness to other theories of intelligence and domain-specific abilities. On a standard bell curve, 130 on the far right is considered to be cognitively or academically gifted. Identification using IQ is problematic for some gifted profiles. Some IQ tests assess a narrow band of culturally valued knowledge, and frequently do not assess general learning capacity. A wide net of evidence needs to be used to drive improvement.

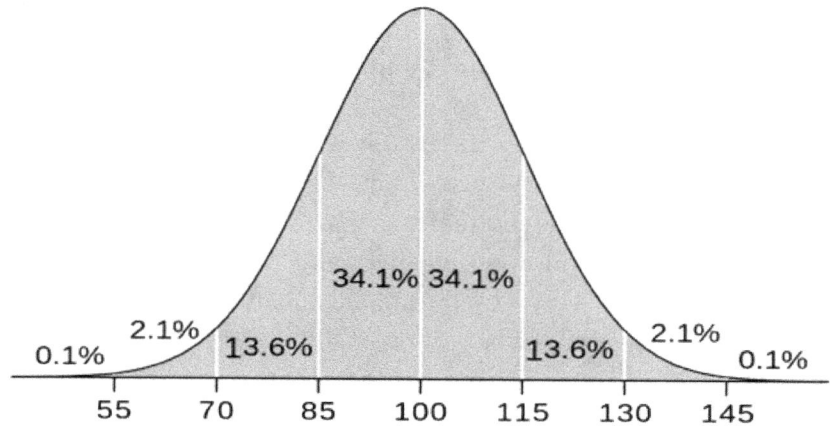

Figure 3: Bell curve of giftedness

Australian state and federal governments support Professor Françoys Gagné's (2005) differentiating model of giftedness and talent (DMGT) renamed in 2018 to the integrative model of talent development (IMTD; 2018). Gagné delineates the gifted as those in the top 10% of natural ability and the talented as those in the top 10% of achievement. The IMTD explores how natural abilities develop, setting the stage for their translation into talents via environmental and intrapersonal catalysts and developmental processes.

Giftedness comes in many forms, as you will see in Gagné's DMGT 2.0 model further in the chapter. We can find giftedness in the visual and performing arts, leadership, sport and many other facets of society. According to Sternberg (1986; Sternberg et al., 2001), some people are more gifted analytically, some creatively, some practically, and some are gifted in more than one area.

Differentiated instruction enables teachers to address learner variance by adjusting the curriculum, materials, learning activities, learning environments and assessments. We will explore gifted students and the need to have their curriculum differentiated in Chapter 2.

INDICATORS OF POSSIBLE GIFTEDNESS IN A SECONDARY SCHOOL SETTING

Gifted secondary school students can demonstrate they are gifted in many ways. What might teachers and parents observe or see in the classroom or at home?

Many gifted secondary students display advanced language skills for their age. Usually gifted students have advanced vocabulary in the secondary school setting.

The creatively gifted student is often gifted in the visual and performing arts sector but they are also the innovators of the time.

A domain-specific gifted relates to a student whose gifts which are focussed in a unique area like sport, leadership or music.

A gifted visual spatial thinking student is often a great problem solver, which may exhibit in mathematics or an engineering subject. These students are sometimes the gifted photographers and virtual game developers of their generation.

The ethno-cultural giftedness is particularly relevant in the Australian setting as both migration and refugee intakes mean that English is often not the first language of the students and this may 'hide' their giftedness.

A major, ongoing issue within the field of gifted education is the underrepresentation of low-income and culturally and linguistically diverse students within gifted programs (Peters & Engerrand, 2016), often attributed to biased teachers and identification practices. This needs an entire chapter of its own and is not just confined to secondary students. Cultural norms can also mask giftedness. Gifted secondary school students will often not be forthcoming in class as they have been taught to not 'stand out'. They are taught at home to respect their elders and teachers. This includes girls from particular cultural backgrounds.

Gifted underachievement is typically defined as a discrepancy between the student's school performance and some index of their ability, such as intelligence, achievement, creativity test scores or ethnographic data. Often the gifted underachieving student will resist challenges, participate reluctantly and strive to belong socially to a peer group. The gifted underachieving student may deny their talent and even be perceived as a compliant but average student. Gifted girls can often underachieve, as they do not want to appear to be smart in front of boys (Kerr, 2013).

It is important to determine the reasons for underachievement in order to tackle it. All too often and for myriad reasons, especially when differentiation is really the answer, gifted students can slip under the radar.

Twice exceptional (2e) gifted students are those who also have a physical disability or who are also on the autism spectrum. In secondary schools, the deficit is often noticed by the teachers before their giftedness. McCoach et al. (2001) define such learners as "students of superior intellectual ability who exhibit a significant discrepancy in their level of performance in a particular academic area such as reading, mathematics, spelling or written expression". Sometimes it is confused with underachievement.

Here is an example of a checklist for gifted students. This one is based on Lannie Kavensky's brilliant behaviours but there are many others available on the Internet.

Characteristic	Descriptor
Humour	Keen sense of the comical, the bizarre or absurd. Pick ups subtleties that others don't notice.
Imagination and creativity	Extraordinary capacity for ingenious, flexible use of ideas, processes, materials etc. Highly original.
Sensitivity	Ususually aware of, or responsive to experiences and feelings; their own and/or others. Empathetic.
Expressiveness	Extraordinary ability to communicate meaning or emotion through words, actions, symbols or media.
Intuition	Suddenly discovers connectins or deeper meaning without conscious awareness of reasoning and thought.
Learning	Grasps and uses sophisticated new understandings quickly and easily.
Moral and ethical concerns	Intense need for firmness and justice. Takes action to resolve injustices. Concerned for the consequences of their actions. Strong sense of right and wrong.
Motivation	Persistent, intense need to know, do, feel, create or understand. Enthusiastic. Perserveres.
Interests	Intense passion, concern, knowledge and/or curiousity about one area or many areas.

Figure 4: Identification checklist for gifted and talented students
(Based on Frasier's core attributes and Kavensky's brilliant behaviours.)

Betts and Neihart revised profiles of giftedness

Betts and Neihart revised profiles of giftedness can be used at staff meetings to identify specific students. It is amazing how teachers find students who require further investigation for giftedness. This table is easy to Google and also comes in A4 pages for each profile.

The key profiles are:

- **Type I – The successful**
  The most well understood of the gifted profiles
  Consumer of knowledge
  Achieves at high level
  Conformist needs challenge
  Can become bored

- **Type II – The creative**
  Divergently gifted
  Often go unidentified
  Bored or frustrated
  Heightened sensitivity
  High tolerance for ambiguity
  Psychologically vulnerable

- **Type III – The underground**
  Middle secondary school females hiding giftedness
  High school boys dealing with athletic or social pressures
  Want to be included in non-gifted peer group
  May be radical transformation from earlier grades
  Their needs are often in conflict with expectations of teachers & parents

- **Type IV – The at risk**
  Probably the most concerning of all the gifted profiles
  Question authority
  Don't conform – haven't learned to use the system
  Receive little recognition for accomplishments
  Struggle with self-esteem
  At risk as eventual drop out

- **Type V – Twice exceptional/The double-labelled**
  Physically or emotionally challenged
  Learning disabilities
  Limited English proficiency
  Typically not identified gifted
  Programs don't integrate their varying needs
  Discouraged, frustrated, rejected, helpless, powerless or isolated
  School system tends to focus on the weaknesses

- **Type VI – The autonomous learner**
  Few demonstrate this at an early age – a definite secondary school trait
  Positive attention and support for accomplishments
  Respected by adults and peers
  Leadership roles
  Independent, self-directed
  Strong, positive self-concept
  Work effectively in school system
  Use the system to create new opportunities

MODELS OF GIFTEDNESS

Françoys Gagné DMGT 2.0

Françoys Gagné (2012) model of giftedness has been adopted in many countries around the world including Australia. His model of giftedness is one of outstanding natural abilities, called aptitudes, in one or more ability domains, to a degree that places an individual in the top 10% of similar-aged peers.

Gagné puts teachers in the driving seat and makes it clear that a child's learning will not progress optimally unless he or she has the ongoing support of the school. If you look at the diagram below you will see that teachers are one of the important catalysts for identifying giftedness. With so many domains of giftedness, the reality is that, 'one size fits all' curriculum is untenable. Differentiation is a necessary tool for teaching all students, but it is a MUST for gifted students. The differences in natural abilities obviously require a different approach to teaching and learning.

One size fits all curriculum does not work when you have a variety of students engage with their learning. When explaining this to secondary teachers I use the Gagné DMGT 2.0 (2012) model printed overleaf.

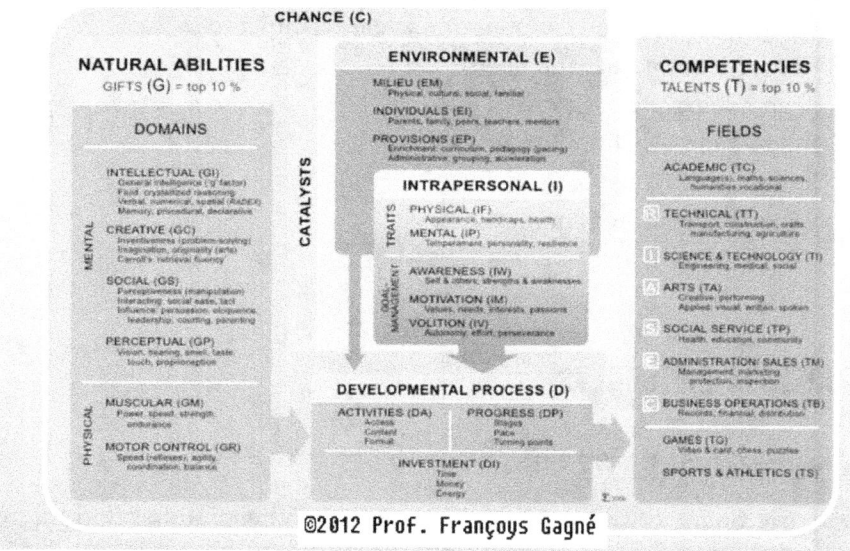

Figure 5: Gagné's DMGT 2.0 model

As educators, it is important to be cognisant of Gagné's model, even his newest model (2018) as we have both the opportunity and the obligation to identify the abilities of the gifted students in our classes and schools; and assist these young people to develop these high abilities into high achievements. It is vital that as educators we understand that students will engage with the curriculum if it is not repetitive and offers appropriate level challenges.

ZPD

Vygotsky (Bruner, 1984) created the concept of the zone of proximal development, often abbreviated as ZPD, which came to be a central part of his theory. Language is the way that a child communicates with others after they are born and they continue to learn by interacting with those around them. Building on his idea of social interaction as the basis for learning, he broached the value of a mentor or teacher in the life of a student. Differentiation occurs in the yellow/middle area only mention it here as it is written about so frequently in texts about differentiation. Usually people's eyes glaze over when you mention it as it sounds intense!

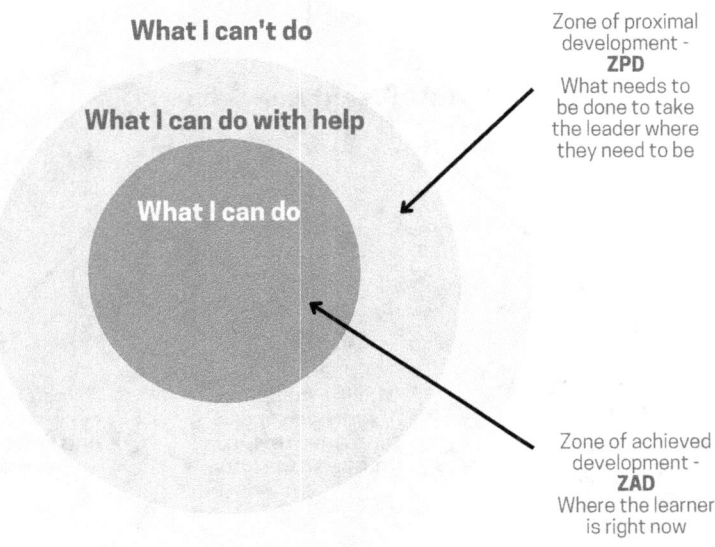

Figure 6: ZPD and ZAD

Sternberg's triarchic theory

The triarchic theory of intelligence proposes that there are three distinct types of intelligence: practical, distinct, and analytical. It was formulated by Robert J. Sternberg, a well-known psychologist whose research often focuses on human intelligence and creativity.

The triarchic theory is also comprised of three subtheories, each of which relates to a specific kind of intelligence: the contextual subtheory, which corresponds to practical intelligence, or the ability to successfully function in one's environment; the experiential subtheory, which corresponds to creative intelligence, or the ability to deal with novel situations or issues; and the componential subtheory, which corresponds to analytical intelligence, or the ability to solve problems.

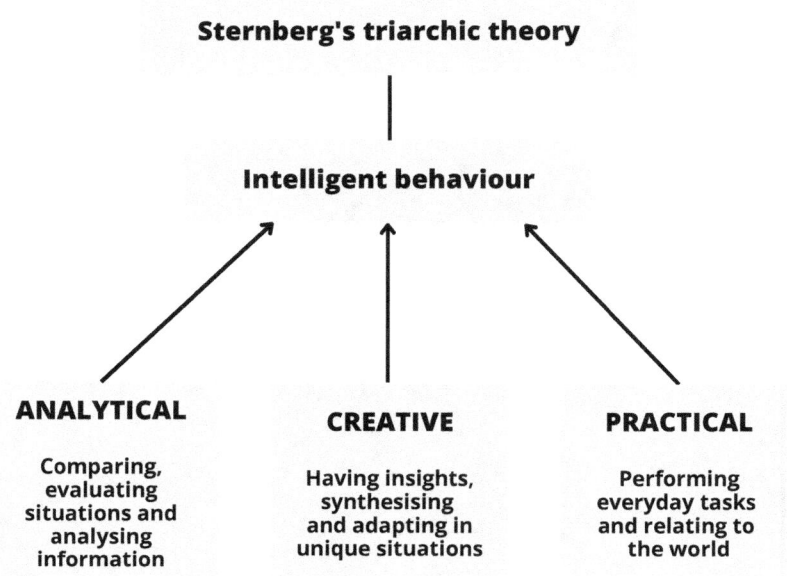

Figure 6: Sternberg's triarchic theory

Sternberg proposed his theory in 1985 as an alternative to the idea of the general intelligence factor. The general intelligence factor, also known as g, is what intelligence tests typically measure and they refer only to 'academic intelligence'.

Sternberg (2001) argued that practical intelligence – a person's ability to react and adapt to the world around them – as well as creativity are equally important when measuring an individual's overall intelligence. He also argued that intelligence isn't fixed, but rather comprises a set of abilities that can be developed. This is an adjunct to Gagné's DMGT 2.0 which refers to intervention needed to bring out the gifted trait.

Transformational giftedness, or giftedness that makes a positive, meaningful, and possibly enduring difference to the world. There are two kinds of transformation that matter: self-transformation and other-transformation. Combining these two kinds of transformation yields a 2 × 2 grid of four kinds of giftedness: non-transformational giftedness (no transformation), transformational giftedness (self- and other-transformation combined), self-realised giftedness (whereby one transforms oneself but not others), and other-realised giftedness (whereby one transforms others but not oneself). This concept is very new and exciting but is still an adjunct to his Triarchic theory.

Renzulli's three-ring conception of giftedness

Jospeh Renzulli thinks gifted behaviour occurs in certain people, at certain times under certain circumstances. He identifies three factors that are important for the development of gifted behaviour: Above average ability, creativity, and task commitment.

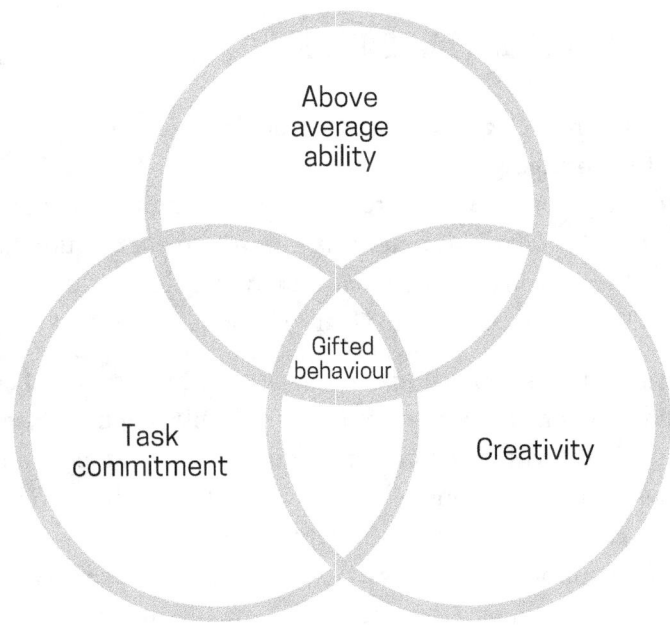

Figure 7: Renzulli's three-ring conception of giftedness (adapted)

The above average abilities Renzulli (2001) purports a difference between general abilities (like processing information, integrating experiences, and abstract thinking) and specific abilities (like the capacity to acquire knowledge, perform in an activity).

By creativity, Renzulli wants us to understand the fluency, flexibility, and originality of thought, an openness to experience, sensitivity to stimulations, and a willingness to take risks.

Under task commitment he understands motivation turned into action (like perseverance, endurance, hard work, but also self-confidence, perceptiveness and a special fascination with a special subject). Renzulli argues that without task commitment, high achievement is simply not possible. Only if characteristics from all three rings work together can high achievement or gifted behaviour be witnessed. The three aspects work together so that the intersection of all three leads to gifted behaviour or the place where gifted students fulfil their potential.

HOW DO THESE THREE MODELS DIFFER?

Renzulli differs from Gagné, as Gagné's model refers to chance or catalysts being vital for bringing giftedness to the surface of the child. Renzulli focusses on three aspects converging in order for giftedness to surface. Recently Renzulli shifted his emphasis toward the background factors in his models, the personality and environmental factors influencing gifted behaviour. This is not contrary to Gagné's model.

Sternberg's own definitions and explanations of his terms and concepts have at times been imprecise, and others think practical intelligence is now redundant with the concept of job knowledge, a concept that is more robust and has been better researched. Sternberg focusses on intelligence as a form of giftedness, while Gagné and Renzulli focus on a broader perception of giftedness. Gagné is a well-respected and widely used model in Australia. Sternberg and Renzulli are often quoted and debated, and are also well respected researchers in the area of giftedness.

Developing curriculum that is sufficiently rigorous, challenging, and coherent for students who are gifted is a challenging task. The result, however, is well worth the effort. Appropriately differentiated curriculum produces well-educated, knowledgeable students who have had to work very hard, have mastered a substantial body of knowledge, and can think clearly and critically about that knowledge. Achieving such results for one or for a classroom full of students who are gifted will produce high levels of satisfaction, not only for the students who are beneficiaries, but also for every teacher who is willing to undertake the challenge.

Differentiation in a secondary school setting is unfortunately not widely debated nor universally implemented. See the next chapter for even more enlightenment.

CHAPTER REFERENCES

Assouline S.G., Colangelo N., VanTassel-Baska J., Lupkowski-Shoplik A., eds. (2015). *A Nation Empowered: Evidence Trumps the Excuses Holding Back America's Brightest Students.* Iowa City, IA: Accel. Inst.

Betts, G. and Neihart, M (2015). Profiles of the Gifted and Talented. Davidson Institute for Talent Development. Reprinted from *Gifted Child Quarterly,* National Association for Gifted Children (NAGC) July.

Bruner, J. (1984). Vygotsky's zone of proximal development: The hidden agenda. *New Directions for Child Development,* 23, 93–97. https://doi.org/10.1002/cd.23219842309

Clark, B. (2008). *Growing up gifted* (7th ed.) Upper Saddle River, NJ: Pearson Prentice Hall.

Csikszentmihalyi, M. (2020). *Finding Flow: The Psychology Of Engagement With Everyday Life Psychology Today.*

Dabrowski, K. (1996). *Multilevelness of emotional and instinctive functions.* Lublin: Towarzystwo Naukowe Katolickiego Uniwersytetu Lubelskiego.

Davis, G. and Rimm, S. (2017). *Education of the gifted and talented.* Prentice-Hall, Inc

Gagné, F. (2004). Transforming gifts into talents: the DMGT as a developmental theory, *High Ability Studies,* 15:2, 119–147.

Gagné, F. (2017). The integrative model of talent development (IMTD): From theory to educational applications. In J. A. Plucker, A. N. Rinn, & M. C. Makel (Eds.), *From giftedness to gifted education: Reflecting theory in practice* (pp. 149–182). Prufrock Press Inc..

Galton F. (1869). Hereditary Genius: An Inquiry Into its Laws and Consequences. Basingstoke, UK: Macmillan

Hallahan, D.P. et al., (2020). *Exceptional Learners.* Oxford Research Encyclopedias, https://oxfordre.com/education/view/10.1093/acrefore/9780190264093.001.0001/acrefor

Jung, J. Y., Barnett, K., Gross, M.U., & McCormick, J. (2011). Levels of intellectual giftedness, culture, and the forced-choice dilemma. *Roeper Review*, 33(3), 182-197.

Kanevsky L. (2013). *The Tool Kit for High End Curriculum Differentiation*. Burnaby, Can.: Simon Fraser University

Kerr, B.A., & McKay, R. (2013). Searching for tomorrow's innovators: Profiling creative adolescents. *Creativity Research Journal*, 25, 21-32. doi: 10.1080/10400419.2013.752180

McCoach D.B., Siegle D. (2001). Factors that differentiate underachieving gifted students from high-achieving gifted students. *Gifted child quarterly* 47 (2), 144-154

Peters S.J., Engerrand K.G., (2016). Equity and excellence: proactive efforts in the identification of underrepresented students for gifted and talented services. *Gifted Child Quarterly*. 60:159-71

Renzulli, J.S. (1997). A practical system for identifying gifted and talented students. *Early Child Development and Care*, 63(1), 9-18

Sternberg, R.J. (2001). ACCEL: a new model for identifying the gifted. *Roeper Review*. 39:152-69

Sternberg, R.J. (1985a). *Beyond IQ: A triarchic theory of human intelligence*. Cambridge, UK: Cambridge University Press

Sternberg, R. J., Chowkase, A., Desmet, O., Karami, S., Landy, J., & Lu, J. (2021). Beyond transformational giftedness. *Education Sciences*, 11(5), 192

CHAPTER 2

MODELS OF DIFFERENTIATION AND HOW TO USE THEM

SUSAN NIKAKIS

Tell me, I'll forget
Show me, I'll remember
Involve me, I'll understand
– Chinese Proverb

The short term goal is to find a template to use for differentiation of the curriculum. The long-term goal might be to use the book as a professional learning enrichment tool or a guide on the side.

Some secondary teachers will be at the beginning of their learning journey about differentiating the curriculum for gifted students, some teachers will want a refresher and some, if not all, hope that they can find an idea easily! Although much has been written about gifted students and differentiation, recent studies show that not much has changed in differentiation practices in the last decade of the last century and the first two of this one (Peters, 2018).

WHAT IS DIFFERENTIATION?

The roots of differentiated instruction go all the way back to the days of the one-room schoolhouse, where one teacher had students of all ages in one classroom. As the educational system transitioned to grading schools, it was assumed that children of the same age learned similarly. However in 1912, achievement tests were introduced, and the scores revealed the gaps in students' abilities within grade levels. Differentiation means that students are able to enter the learning from different levels. Just as diving boards have different levels of difficulty, so too tasks can vary in their level of complexity.

In too many school settings, little differentiation of the curriculum or instruction for gifted secondary school students is provided during the school day and minimal 'enrichment' opportunities are offered. All too often if a secondary student is accelerated in a subject then the 'differentiation' box has apparently been ticked. If students had a choice of activities regardless of the levels of questioning then this too was viewed as differentiation.

The development of a differentiated curriculum for the gifted is difficult and demanding, but so is all quality teaching. Gifted students have a right to have their curriculum differentiated!

WHY DO GIFTED SECONDARY STUDENTS NEED DIFFERENTIATION?

Just as a student who finds the classroom material overwhelming may zone out or misbehave, so too may a gifted student. Even worse, when students who are gifted are routinely unchallenged, they may never learn how to learn. Gifted students need opportunities to analyse, evaluate, create, and reflect. They should gain experience by asking and investigating complex questions and completing challenging tasks.

Although we are focusing on differentiated instruction for gifted students, it is important to note that the strategies discussed in this chapter can apply to all populations of students. "Differentiation is meeting the needs of learners where they are at," says Beasley. "It's a philosophy – not a bag of tricks or a strategy. It's about thinking about the pieces we can differentiate by readiness, by interest, by learning profile, and so on, for whatever type of learners are in your class."

The educational implications of differentiation

For learners
- Need quality links
- Think about more knowledge at once
- Form higher level inferences or extensions and syntheses

For teachers. During a differentiated lesson we should hear
- I think this is like ...
- It reminds me of ...
- This is about ... (drawing out the main idea).

Sometimes I write these sentence starters on the board.

Adjusting the curriculum

Differentiation (Perez, 2016) is certainly getting a lot of buzz lately, but there is no magic wand needed to integrate differentiation into your lesson planning. Quite simply, differentiation is adjusting your instruction to meet the unique needs of your diverse learners.

Furthermore, according to Tomlinson (2001), "Differentiating instruction means 'shaking up' what goes on in the classroom so that students have multiple options for taking in information, making sense of ideas, and expressing what they learn." Differentiation is not a single strategy, but an approach to instruction that incorporates a variety of strategies.

When teachers differentiate, they do so in response to a student's readiness, interest, and learning profile. Because of their unique and diverse literacy needs, our students need us to differentiate the product, process, and/or content of learning.

Differentiation can assist with a diversity of abilities not just gifted students.

Curriculum differentiation refers to adapting the usual curriculum in order to meet an individual student's specific learning needs; curriculum objectives, teaching methods, assessment methods, resources and learning activities are carefully planned to cater for the specific individual needs of students (Kronborg & Plunkett 2008). When we differentiate, we simply offer students opportunities to think and learn at a level appropriate to their ability. In an ideal world, our materials would come with lessons commensurate with students' abilities, but often that's not the case.

An effective curriculum for gifted students is essentially a core curriculum that has been adjusted to meet their various learning needs (Tomlinson & McTighe 2006). Often, highly able students learn more quickly than others their age. As a result, they typically need a more rapid instructional pace than do many of their peers. Students access content at different levels of understanding, just like diving boards can be used to access a pool at different levels. That being said, even the gifted group will have individual differences.

The benefits of differentiation in the classroom are often accompanied by the often perceived drawback of an ever-increasing workload for secondary teachers. Here are a few factors to keep in mind to assist teachers:

Differentiation is not ...
- Asking every student to read the same text with the same purpose and using the same strategy
- Giving the same instruction and assignments to the whole class
- Giving extra assignments to students who finish early
- Individualised instruction for each student

- Doing something completely different for each student in your classroom
- Creating permanent, labelled groups that never change

However:
- Research shows differentiated instruction is effective for high-ability students as well as students with mild to severe disabilities.
- When students are given more options on how they can learn material, they take on more responsibility for their own learning.
- Students appear to be more engaged in learning, and there are reportedly fewer discipline problems in classrooms where teachers provide differentiated lessons.

Differentiation is ...
- Providing different students with different learning experiences
- Based on the students' needs
- Considering students' readiness levels, interests, and learning styles
- A flexible approach to instruction and grouping
- Providing more than one option to the students as they read their texts
- Using different reading strategies to match the material to meet the literacy needs of our students
- Changing the way we teach so that everyone can learn and achieve

However:
- Differentiated instruction requires more work during lesson planning, and many teachers struggle to find the extra time in their schedule. (Once you start to share the workload with your colleagues the workload is actually less)
- The learning curve can be steep and some schools lack professional development resources. (This text can help with this challenge).

THE TOMLINSON MODEL OF DIFFERENTIATION

In education circles, Carol Ann Tomlinson is known as the guru of differentiation. The term differentiated instruction was introduced in the late 1990s by Tomlinson (2021), who describes differentiation as instruction so powerful because it focuses on concepts and principals instead of just facts and content. This graphic is good to unpack at a staff meeting.

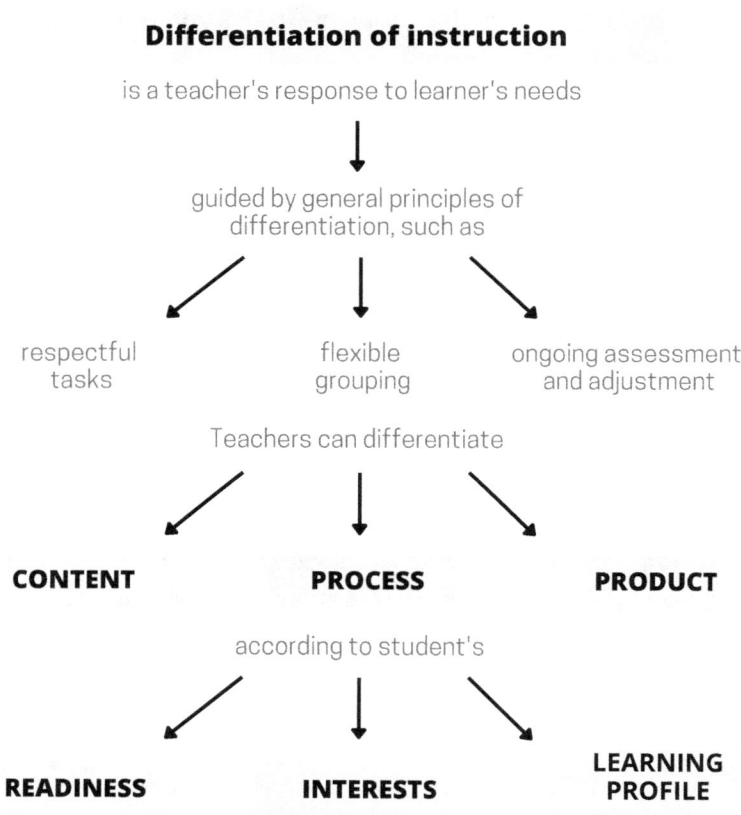

Figure 1: Differentiation of instruction by Tomlison (adapted)

Ways to differentiate

1. **Create a differentiated learning environment**
   The first differentiation technique changes up the physical layout of the classroom. Organise your classroom into flexible workstations. This will require you to move furniture around to support both individual and group work. For example, you can create a teaching table where teacher-led instruction will take place. This workstation would be focused on teaching new, challenging material.

2. **Prepare thoughtful lessons backed by data**
   Before you even begin teaching each lesson, you should examine past assessments, collected data, work samples and student observations to identify specific instructional strengths for each student. Then you can change the process of the learning experience by assigning different tasks to different learners. A good way to differentiate the learning process is to have a series of tiered assignments for each of your lessons. By creating a variety of related tasks at varying difficulty, you'll be able to give specific tasks to certain groups or individual students based on their skill level. They can then work their way up to the highest assignment. You'll want to make sure that you're continually assessing students' progress and providing them with relevant feedback that will help them work towards their educational goals. Interrogating data can be a challenge but can give you a fuller picture of a students strengths.

3. **Tailor assignments based on students' learning goals**
   Using differentiation strategies to shake up the end product that students turn in for assignments can also help you reach different learners. You can offer students different avensue to present their understanding of the lesson based on how they learn the material. For example, some learners may want to create a poster to show their understanding of Newton's first law of motion (inertia) while some may prefer to write a paper or some may want to give an oral presentation.

4. **Switch the content up**

   Use computer programs, tape recordings, videos or even making it an interactive lesson by having students act out scenes from the play. Remember, it's important to keep your eyes and ears open when using differentiated instruction. You'll need to constantly assess how your efforts are affecting your students while keeping the discussion open and engagement high. Differentiated instruction takes a lot of planning, but with continuous assessment and varying strategies, you'll be able to accommodate all of your students' learning profiles.

5. **Build a learning profile**

   Tomlinson (2014) also gives teachers advice on differentiated instruction using students' learning profile. I have found that using Howard Gardner's theory of multiple intelligences assists with creating a profile of how a student prefers to learn. Tomlinson points out that is respectful to cater for the learning needs of our students but it also makes differentiation even easier. Student choice is very important and using multiple intelligences add to your basket of differentiation strategies.

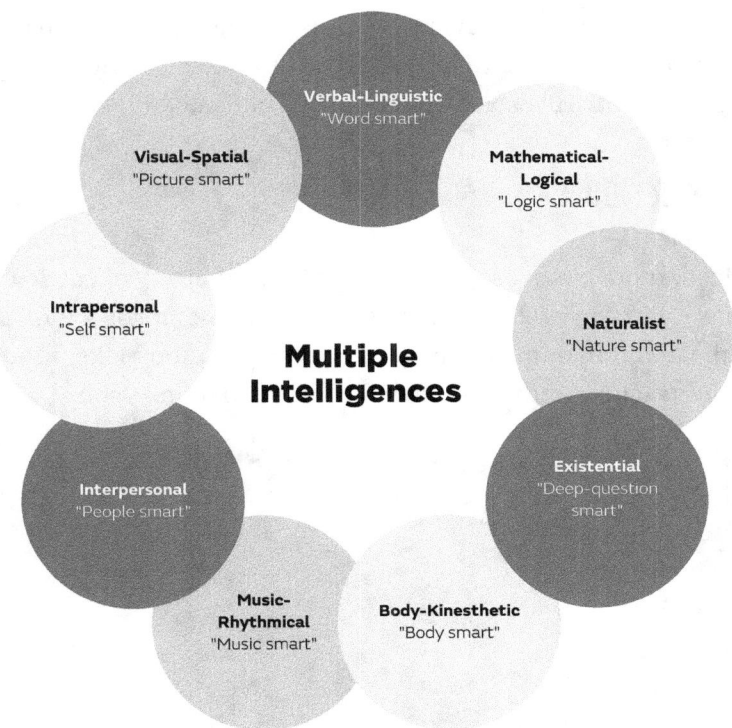

Figure 2: Howard Gardner's multiple intelligences

The differentiation philosophy indicates that students become stronger learners when they can accept more responsibility for their own learning and when they become more proficient in understanding their goals, their status relative to those goals, and how to adjust their approach to learning in order to achieve the goals. Students enjoy the multiple intelligences test too.

Google a multiple intelligences test and give it to the students. Whether you are a teacher or a student who is curious, this multiple intelligence test printable will help you identify a person's strongest intelligences. A multiple intelligence quiz for students can be a valuable resource to help children develop and learn to the best of their abilities. Teachers can develop and use classroom activities designed for multiple intelligences. Different children learn differently, which is why you need classroom activities for multiple intelligences. Students who don't learn traditionally may be left behind by regular classwork. By engaging students in multiple intelligence activities that teach to each of the eight different types of intelligences, you will be able to help all of your students succeed.

THE MAKER MODEL

The Maker model is an easy way to explain the delivery of curriculum to students. You can easily see the overlap with Tomlinson's model. I do think the addition of the learning environment in the Maker model is a bonus for teachers' organisation of the differentiation lesson.

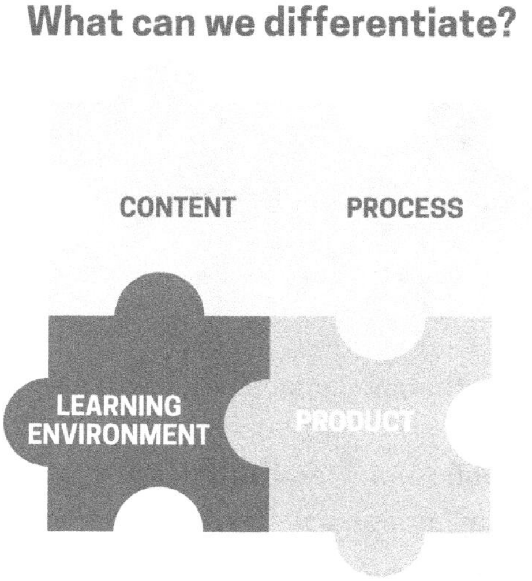

Figure 2: Maker model of curriculum differentiation

June Maker's (2010) model of states that differentiation should occur in the following areas:
- **Content**, the content should be modified in terms of its level of complexity, variety and organisation.
- **Process**, the process should be varied by presenting students with higher order thinking skills including creative, analytical and evaluative questions. Open-ended thinking questions should be included ensuring that students also have freedom of choice of the way they record their responses.

- **Products** should be modified to include real-world problems, real-world audiences, real deadlines and transformations.
- **Learning environments** should be modified to include opportunities for student-centred learning, independence opportunities plus varied groupings possibilities.

Here it is in a box with each noun elaborated upon. Sometimes I place a large sized laminated copy of this is my subject room. If you teach your students about this model they can actually begin to design the questions and construct the assessment rubrics. What powerful learning.

Content	Process
Content should be modifed in terms of its level of: • Abstraction • Complexity • Vareity • Organisation As well as involving the: • Study of people • Study of methods of inquiry.	Process should be modified in terms of the: • Higer order thiking skills – analysis, synthesis and evaluation • Open-ended thinking – paradox, analogy, intiuitive expression, tolerance for ambiguity As well as involving: • Discovery • Proof and reasoning • Freedom of choice • Group interactions
Product	**Learning environment**
Products should be modified to include: • Real-world problems • Real-world audiences • Real deadlines • Evaluation • Transformations.	The learning environment should be modified to include opportunities for: • Student-centred learning • Independence • Openess • Acceptance • Complexity in setting • Varied groupings • High mobility.

Figure 4: Maker model of curriculum differentiation explained

Differentiation is not streaming

A number of writers over the years have tried to equate differentiation with streaming. As we are addressing the differentiation of gifted secondary school students we need to define differentiation as it pertains to individual subject areas found specifically in the majority of secondary school. Differentiation can be the exploration of a particular theme using a research based inquires approach. This is giving the students choice of presentation and depth of information. Placing gifted students in a group within a mixed ability classroom is not streaming.

BLOOM'S TAXONOMY

Traditionally however, differentiation was understood to be Benjamin Bloom's (1956) idea using a taxonomy of critical thought. Bloom's taxonomy is a hierarchical ordering of cognitive skills which can help students to learn at a level appropriate to their understanding. Teachers designed questions and outcomes which were aimed at a knowledge level for the students grappling with a theme or concept. There are usually six levels even in Bloom's revised taxonomy (Anderson and Krathwohl, 2001) with creating now the top level. This taxonomy allowed students to choose from one of six areas of difficulty with each level containing a greater depth of knowledge and understanding. The revised taxonomy can be used to create assessments where the student can achieve success. Instead of giving the weaker swimmer 50 metres to complete, these students would be asked to swim five metres. Yes they could see other students being offered greater challenges but they could aim to improve their swimming thus moving up the taxonomy. We now have Bloom's revised (2010) taxonomy. The top three levels are best for gifted students.

```
        CREATING            EVALUATING           ANALYSING
        Use info to       Critically examine   Take info apart
          create            info and make        and explore
      something new          judgements         relationships

                             APPLYING
                          Use info in a new
                          (but similar) form

                           UNDERSTANDING
                          Use info in a new
                          (but similar) form

                            REMEMBERING
                              Find or
                             remember
                               info
```

Figure 5: Using Bloom's taxonomy for effective learning
(adapted from Lewis, 2020)

Boring old Bloom who is simply misunderstood and misused!

Each level of the pyramid has a corresponding verb. You use the verb to construct the question.

1. The first level of Bloom's taxonomy is to **Remember**.
   Example activities at the Remembering level are; to memorise a poem, recall state capitals, and remember math formulas. Often this level of Bloom's taxonomy is used as a pretest for students.

2. The second level of Bloom's taxonomy is to **Understand**.
   Activities at the Understanding level are to organise the animal kingdom based on a given framework, illustrate the difference between a rectangle and square, and summarize the plot of a simple story.

3. The third level of Bloom's taxonomy is to **Apply**.
   Activities at the Application level are use a formula to solve a problem, select a design to meet a purpose and reconstruct the passage of a new law through a given government system.

4. The fourth level of Bloom's taxonomy is to **Analyse**.
   Activities at the Analysis level could to be to identify the 'parts of' democracy, explain how the steps of the scientific process work or, identify why a machine isn't working

5. The fifth level of Bloom's taxonomy is to **Evaluate**.
   Example activities at the Evaluation level are to make a judgement regarding an ethical dilemma or interpreting the significance of a given law of physics. This level could also include illustrating the relative value of a technological innovation in a specific setting like farming.

6. The sixth and final level of Bloom's taxonomy is to **Create**.
   This level is only a recent addition and it reflect changes in educators approach to learning and teaching, Examples at the Creation level include design a new solution to an 'old' problem which acknowledges the previous failures, delete the least useful arguments in a persuasive essay or write a poem based on a given theme. Create is the highest level of Bloom's revised taxonomy. It means to compile information together in a different way by combining elements in a new pattern or proposing alternative solutions. Create is a wonderful level for gifted students.

How to do make Bloom work in the classroom?

Teachers can then design instructional activities to cover each of the six levels of thinking (Kendrick, 2007).

Many gifted students learn best when they can work with something tangible. Therefore, try to think of activities that will enable them to get 'down and dirty' with the material.

If we look at this most widely recognised of the taxonomies we see that it can be used for project based learning with choice for students, or as a hierarchy for students to work towards or work through. Some teachers believe that Bloom's taxonomy is not a tool which can be used at the secondary school level and although it certainly is only one way of differentiation the fact is, that it can be used as a basis for lesson planning at any year level.

Bloom's revised taxonomy with an example for a secondary class

A Shakespearean play can seem overwhelming with its advanced content, unless you like use a tool like Bloom's revised taxonomy (2010) to make it more palatable to our secondary school students. Here are some examples:
- List the main characters' names in Romeo and Juliet. That's the bottom of the Bloom's taxonomy which is remember or identify. This is asking a low-level question.
- An in-depth question in the create section could be compare and contrast the Montague and Capulet families with Australian federal politics. How are power and deceit portrayed to the audience?
- Dr Seuss can also have every level of Bloom's taxonomy but an in-depth or create question could be: (remember that the concept of power needs to be explored first in an 'understand' question.)
- "Evaluate the ethical use of power in The Cat in the Hat and compare it to the use of power in Green Eggs and Ham. In which story is power used more dangerously?" Here, despite the seemingly low level of content (Dr Seuss), the thinking (evaluate; compare and contrast) required makes an interesting question even for secondary students.

To truly differentiate, we have four focus areas: increase thinking skills, adjust the level of content, provide sufficiently interesting resources, and design an appropriate product.

As a teacher, once I started pre-assessing using the bottom of Bloom's taxonomy, I quickly discovered that many of my students already knew a great deal about what I was planning teaching them. Recent research shows that this is surprisingly common (Gagné, 2018). Planning using the knowledge gained from the pre-assessments is time consuming when you first embark on a differentiation journey but once you become adept at writing various levels of questions it makes teaching and learning an exciting place to be.

The development of a differentiated curriculum for the gifted is difficult and demanding, but so is all quality teaching. Gifted students have a right to have their curriculum differentiated.

I love the use of verbs and quite often ask my students to help me write the questions. You have to ensure that they understand the meanings of all the verbs. This sounds like 'outsourcing your lesson planning' but it is powerful teaching and learning.

If my class reads about the Ballarat gold rush and then I suggest they create either a poem, a presentation, or a short play, there is no differentiated instruction happening.

If most of my class is learning the basic facts about the Ballarat gold rush using a set textbook, I'm going to purposefully plan a task to push my gifted students. This means adjusting thinking skills, content, process and learning environment (see the Maker model of differentiation). Perhaps they'll compare and contrast with the San Francisco gold rush and then form an opinion about which process for accessing the gold is the more efficient model. This is content and thinking skill.

When we differentiate, it needs to be about students' thinking. A great test is: does this challenge the student to the point that they need a little help?

As educators it is our responsibility to differentiate lessons for students of varying abilities. Gifted students ultimately require lessons centred on the upper level. They also require limited revision and lots of reflection time.

To truly differentiate, we must increase thinking skills, adjust the level of content, provide sufficiently interesting resources, and design an appropriate product that shows off students' learning. When planning a lesson, we have to not just differentiate content (which is what the prompts of depth and complexity do), but also adjust the thinking that we expect students to do. What do your students need to know? What is the driving question? (Munro, 2013). We also need to listen to our students so we can facilitate in-depth inquiry.

Nothing stirs up behaviour problems like trying to teach a gifted student something they already know. It is important to remember however that just because a student is gifted, doesn't mean they have mastered every skill in the various domains. Differentiation is underpinned by the principle that all children can learn when teachers use a variety of methods and when students have choice in how they demonstrate their learning. Differentiation is not a fad. Adapting the language and pace of instruction and providing a range of options for students to demonstrate their learning is the essence of quality teaching.

HOW TO TARGET DIFFERENT SENSES AND LEARNING PROFILES WITHIN DIFFERENTIATED LESSONS

Rethink how lessons can be presented using a range of learning profiles by:
- Playing video clips
- Using infographics
- Providing audiobooks
- Using creative dramatics and role-play to act out scenes of a story
- Using charts and illustrations with text
- Providing verbal and written directions to tasks
- Using real and other physical objects to explain key concepts
- Allowing time for artistic reflections and symbolic summaries by encouraging students to;
    - Perform dance routines to act out historical or literary events
    - Create songs or raps about math concepts
    - Perform sound and vibration experiments in science
    - Dramatically re-enact historical or literary events
    - Run mock political campaigns and elections

Make time for journaling and quick-write activities.

Don't be afraid to press the pause button and have students reflect on the lessons you've taught or stories they have read.

Points to note
- Differentiation is providing challenges at different levels for different students.
- Differentiation is different, not more!
- Differentiation does not equal acceleration into a higher level.

So taking diversity into account by planning from the outset is not only better for students and teachers, but it saves time and is easier and more successful than a 'one size fits all' approach.

FAVOURITE MODELS OF DIFFERENTIATION

While there are many methods and models of differentiation the following are some of the most widely popular when used in a classroom situation.

The three story intellect

My favourite differentiation tool is this version from Art de Costa who borrowed it from Oliver Wendell Holmes who based it on Bloom's taxonomy. I write leading questions utilising the verbs in each story, Level one can be used for students who are struggling with a topic or them or it can be used for pretesting questions. The middle level is accessible to most students and the top level is for higher order thinkers. Occasionally I encourage my students to choose their own level however the downside is that you might miss your gifted underachievers.

Use the verbs as question stimulators. The three story intellect is just a variation of Bloom's taxonomy. There are many variations of this house on the internet I think this is clear for students and easy to understand.

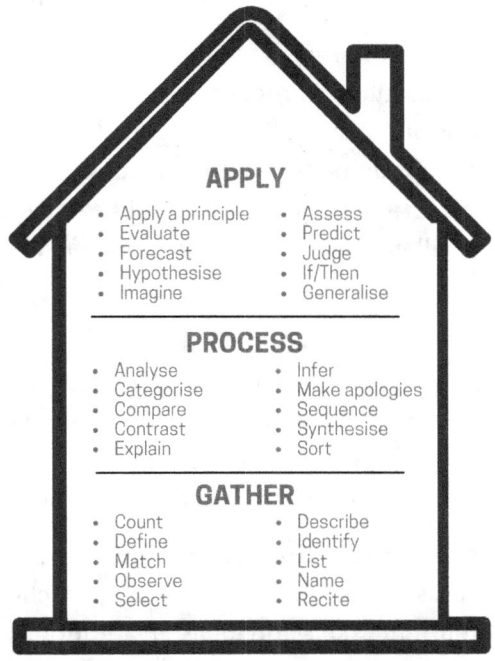

Figure 6: Costa's three-story intellect

How to use this version in a classroom?
Just copy it, fold it in half vertically and students are ready to ask questions or write questions. I love the use of flapbooks in student journals or student interactive notebooks. Flapbooks are versatile tools for taking notes or as quick formative assessments. The top story verbs are for the gifted students.

How do you start a level 3 question?
Level three questions go beyond the text, yet must show an understanding of the ideas in the text. These questions typically require reasoning, complexity, and/or planning. If it's a level three question, you explain/justify your thinking and provide supporting evidence for reasoning or conclusions you make.

Six ways to differentiate instruction for gifted students

- **Create tiered assignments**
  Tiered assignments allow learners to complete the same assignment at different levels of difficulty. By varying the level of difficulty, you're letting each student demonstrate understanding. Some teachers do this by designing an assignment for the middle tier and then adding in an additional challenge for students who are gifted. For example, you could ask gifted students to apply a skill in two ways instead of one.

- **Allow gifted students to work at their own pace**
  Perhaps there's an independent project related to the topic that a gifted learner could work on, or maybe the student could skip some of the earlier assignments. How about letting the gifted students work on two assignments at once or giving them fewer directions?

- **Offer open-ended or self-directed assignments and activities**
  Open-ended tasks can have many valid approaches, and students can apply their unique skills and ideas. In addition, an activity that is open-ended can stimulate higher-order thinking. Let gifted learners be responsible for their own development by giving them a say in how far they take their own learning. Ask higher-level questions and encourage students to offer creative responses, work in pairs to question each other, and find ways to stimulate further exploration. You may even allow your students who are gifted to work on an independent study in an interest area whenever they have free time.

- **Compact the curriculum**
  Compacting refers to tossing out the part of the lesson that students already know, which frees them up to work on something more challenging. In a math class, for example, you might choose the essential problems that demonstrate mastery. If students can correctly solve those problems, they can move on to an extension activity.

- **Deliver project-based learning**
  Project based learning (PBL) is a teaching method in which students gain knowledge and skills by working for an extended period of time to investigate and respond to an authentic, engaging, and complex question, problem, or challenge.

- **Pair gifted students up**
  Allowing students who are gifted to work together in small groups boosts their achievement because they challenge themselves. Academic competition is important for gifted students to learn how to deal with success and defeat. In fact, academic competitions that are designed to entice students to work independently or in teams; this kind of work helps gifted students handle pressure and gain experience in real-life challenges. When you let gifted students work together, they can work on advanced content or assignments at their level. Because students can be talented in different ways, you can use this strategy to help them learn from each other and expand their horizons.

Teaching and stimulating thinking by asking questions is often called the 'Socratic method'. Paul (1992) organised 'Socratic questions' which elicit clarifying and analysing assumptions, probing reasons and evidence, analysing viewpoints or perspectives, analysing implications and consequences and questioning. The taxonomy of socratic questions category *Questions about the Questions* includes such higher order questions a lot like the American 'Jeopardy' TV program.

'To answer this question, what questions would we have to answer first?'

For example. Lady Macbeth was one of his most manipulative characters. Answer = Who is Shakespeare?

The students love learning variation.

So differentiation is:
- Adjusting the content, process, product, and environment to meet the specific educational needs of each student. The environment includes the child's social and emotional needs.
- An approach that benefits all students including gifted students
- Curriculum instruction and assessment that is carefully designed to meet the needs of all
- Student centred

In other words ...
- Differentiation is responsive teaching rather than one-size-fits-all teaching.

Differentiation is most certainly a concept which secondary school teachers should incorporate into their lesson planning for gifted students. According to Reis (1990b), teachers need a plan. This plan should consist of well thought out lists (taxonomies) of skills, a timetable for teaching them, and effective teaching techniques.'

There is also another 'urban legend' that secondary school teachers do not have time to differentiate the curriculum therefore all students are taught content simultaneously. One size fits all again!

MAKING IT EASIER FOR TEACHERS

One of the benefits which can be used at the secondary level is the number of teachers taking the same course. There are at least two year 8 teachers of English, therefore those teachers can split the preparation of the unit between them. Usually, there are at least two school teaches and often up to eight in larger secondary schools. This is ideal for sharing the differentiation load. The teachers can then choose to prepare one section of the differentiation plan. This is a very efficient use of resources and works well when people share the load. It is not more work for the teacher, just higher level in depth question creating. This allows the teachers to really differentiate and drill right down to a question.

Keep in mind an acronym for remembering grouping alternatives for differentiation TAPS (Perez, 2016):
- **T** = Total group instruction
- **A** = Alone time
- **P** = Partner work
- **S** = Small-group work

I always write this on the board or computer so my students begin to understand the different ways of responding to the differentiated ways of learning.

Different not more

There are many advantages of differentiation of the curriculum for gifted students, however it is important that is that the following suggestions are NOT made to these students.
1. Just read your book or
2. Go and help another student or
3. Do more problems or
4. Use more colours!

Let us look at these anti-differentiation practices one by one. There's nothing wrong with reading a book, but reading by yourself is not differentiated instruction. You can read a book by yourself in bed at home, floating in a pool, or at the beach. We should expect more from school than recreational reading. Rather than independently reading until the class concludes, students should participate in a task or lesson purposefully structured, one with a clear learning goal and success criteria that makes sense for that student. If told to go off and 'read a book' there is no instruction, no higher order thinking, no opportunity to discuss with the teacher, and no learning other than what the child teaches themselves.

Go and help another student! Gifted students are not mini teachers. There's a reason athletic superstars rarely become great coaches and superstar coaches were rarely the best athletes. A student who finishes quickly often 'gets it' in the same way that Ash Barty 'gets' tennis. Neither are necessarily going to be good at teaching it. While teaching something to somebody else is a good way of reinforcing learning, our gifted students do not need that either. Teaching is a skill unto itself, also teaching students is the teacher's job, not the students. If you took an evening cooking class and ended up teaching the other students, you'd probably ask for your money back. Each student deserves a task or lesson that is meaningfully challenging to them. Having your gifted student help other students is NOT differentiation of the curriculum. These students should be learning at a level that is appropriate to them, not teaching their peers.

More work and not different work is the Achilles heel for gifted students. This often happens when a student finishes earlier than expected and, as 'differentiation', gets more of the same, another worksheet to complete or more problems to finish.

The 'use more colours' is another way to fill in time for gifted students with some particularly naive teachers. Those perfectionist gifted students will usually think that their effort is not good enough but they may well just throw the work which was already very good in the bin! So much for differentiation! Teachers need to distinguish decoration from differentiation.

What differentiation isn't!

Choice is often confused with differentiation. Just because students are doing different things doesn't mean that differentiated instruction is part of this choice.

The following is a list you can debate at a staff meeting to raise awareness of differentiating for gifted secondary students. Discuss with your colleagues the reasons the following points are indeed myths.

Myth	Gifted students don't need help; they'll do fine on their own
Myth	Teachers challenge all the students, so gifted kids will be fine in the regular classroom
Myth	Gifted students make everyone else in the class smarter by providing a role model or a challenge
Myth	All children are gifted
Myth	Acceleration placement options are socially harmful for gifted students
Myth	Gifted education programs are elitist
Myth	That student can't be gifted, he is receiving poor grades
Myth	Gifted students are happy, popular, and well adjusted in school
Myth	This child can't be gifted, as he has a disability
Myth	Gifted education requires an abundance of resources

Research has highlighted curriculum differentiation as a key strategy for providing appropriate access to learning for gifted students. For example, Monash and Federation University gifted education experts, Kronborg and Plunkett (2008) have found that "while a number of requirements appear to be vital to any successful programmatic response to meeting the needs of high ability students, curriculum differentiation inevitably emerges as perhaps the most important of all".

Another great tool (but you need some experience before you embark on this) is Kanevsky's (2013) *The Tool Kit for High End Curriculum Differentiation*. This is a free computer program which uses his brilliant behaviours as a basis for planning differentiation.

Differentiating instruction enables teachers to respond to the diversity of abilities, levels of giftedness, learning needs and interests of gifted students. The aim is to ensure each student is challenged and supported to grow in knowledge, skills and understanding across the curriculum domains. In this way, each student has the opportunity to exceed beyond their potential and aspirations (Hattie, 2012).

So this chapter has provided you with models, examples and philosophies of education related to differentiation. There are many more if you Google differentiation ideas but I have also included some additional references which you might find useful after the formal ones used in this chapter.

CHAPTER REFERENCES

Anderson, L.W., & Krathwohl, D.R. (2001). *A taxonomy for learning, teaching, and assessing*, Abridged Edition. Boston, MA: Allyn and Bacon

Bloom, B.S. (1956). *Taxonomy of educational objectives: The classification of educational goals. Handbook I: Cognitive domain.* New York: Longmans, Green

Gagné, F. (2018). The DMGT: Changes within, beneath, and beyond, *Talent Development & Excellence*, 5 (1), 5–19

Hattie, J. (2012). *Visible Learning for Teachers: Maximizing Impact on Learning*, Routledge, New York

Kanevsky, L. (2013). *The Tool Kit for High End Curriculum Differentiation.* Burnaby, Can.: Simon Fraser University

Kronborg, L. & Plunkett, M. (2008). Curriculum differentiation: An innovative Australian secondary school program to extend academic talent, *Australasian Journal of Gifted Education*, 17 (1), 19–29

Lewis, B. (2020). *Using Bloom's Taxonomy for Effective Learning*. ThoughtCo, thoughtco.com/blooms-taxonomy-the-incredible-teaching-tool-2081869

Munro, J. (2013). Gifted students as expert knowers: A teaching friendly model of gifted knowing and understanding? *CSE Seminar series 225*. Mercer House, East Melbourne

Maker, C.J., Schiever, S.W. (2010). *Curriculum development and teaching strategies for gifted learners* (3 rd Ed.) Pro-Ed

OECD (2019). Education Policy Outlook (2019). *Working Together to Help Students Achieve their Potential,* OECD Publishing, Paris, https://doi.org/10.1787/2b8ad56e-en

Paul, R. (1992). *Critical thinking: What every person needs to survive in a rapidly changing world*. Rohnert Park, C.A; Foundation for Critical thinking

Peters, S. J., & Jolly, J. L. (2018). The influence of professional development in gifted education on the frequency of instructional practices. *The Australian Educational Researcher,* 45(4), 473–491

Perez, K. (2016). *200+ proven strategies for teaching reading*. Bloomington, IN: Solution Tree Press

Reis, S. M. (1990). What to teach, when to teach it. *Learning,* 90, 46-47

Tomlinson, C. (2014). *The differentiated classroom: Responding to the needs of all learners* (2nd ed.). Alexandria, VA: Association for the Supervision of Curriculum Development

Tomlinson, C.A. (2021). *So Each May Soar: The principles and practices of learner-centred classrooms*. Alexandra, Virginia: ASCD

CHAPTER 3

WHAT ELSE IS AVAILABLE FOR GIFTED SECONDARY STUDENTS?

MARK SMITH

By the time gifted students enter the secondary educational setting many are far more selective about what they will engage with. A good primary gifted program will hopefully have set the scene for personal skill, knowledge development and engagement with challenge. It will have delivered a range of opportunities to diversely gifted students and developed an ongoing love of learning through direct teaching, process learning, collaborative group work, a range of creative elements, and many varied challenges and independent tasks. By the end of the primary program gifted students should have a level of passion, drive and autonomy. They should have developed a positive approach to education and have a well-established work routine aligning with their abilities. They may have some degree of specialisation that they wish to explore and further develop. This might provide significant direction for their secondary program, or even direct their university aspirations or vocational pathways.

With this independent thought in mind, educators must cater for the next stage of development for secondary students knowing that these gifted children will enter secondary classrooms from a broad range of primary experiences. Many will want to ensure success in the mainstream classroom, so will fiercely protect their 'A' grades. Many will be interested in extending their strengths, but they will need to be excited and motivated by the possibilities to do so. Where their primary gifted program was more general in nature, secondary students will be looking for specifics that align with their skills and passions, and they might 'cherry pick' from what is on offer.

Secondary gifted students will be looking at programs with purpose: programs that offer relevance and skill development for a 21st-century future, and programs that are worth engaging in above and beyond their mainstream course. Without a well thought out set of relevant and purposeful offerings gifted students will likely not engage in a program that they may perceive as extra work for little benefit.

SO, WHAT ELSE IS AVAILABLE FOR SECONDARY GIFTED STUDENTS?

Considering relevance, suitable skill and knowledge development, and what can provide purpose for secondary students, we need to firstly seek input from the students themselves about what they need and want. This provides them with a voice and encourages them to make choices about what they might do to support their broader mainstream programs.

Fredricks et al. (2010) calls these essential elements for increasing highly capable students' interest and passion in academics. Fredricks highlights five key considerations:
- Cognitively complex tasks that are meaningful and challenging
- Posing and solving real problems

- Opportunities to incorporate outside interests and future plans
- Choice over the kinds of activities they work on
- Some control over how they complete tasks

With Fredricks five key considerations in mind, consider Case Study 1 which encompasses a range of Fredricks essential elements in a school-based year 9 program.

CASE STUDY I

Once students enter secondary school their independence demands an opportunity for their voice to be heard and their choices to be considered. Voice and choice become key to their initial engagement and their future selections. For many years my colleagues and I have used interviews and surveys at the start of the school year to seek student input and direct programs. Even when I was running primary gifted programs, as a result of interviews and surveys of the students, new program elements were added. Two early ones were algebraic problem-solving maths, and community projects. These were added purely due to the number of primary gifted students who wanted to explore these disciplines.

There are a strong links between giving students choices and their intrinsic motivation for doing a task, their overall performance on the task, and their willingness to accept challenging tasks. Since becoming a secondary teacher of the gifted and a program developer, student voice and choice has determined the broader program. Consequently, all of our secondary programs start the year with a student survey that is different at each year level. The survey is developed from student interviews the previous year and asks the students to select from program units each term, so four options in the four-term year, and a competition/advancement each term, again with four choice options in the four-term year.

The year 9 survey with offerings can be seen in figure 1 and 2 overleaf.

Program Units
Throughout the year students will have the option to participate in a variety of program units and competitions as a part of Dare2Dream!, the extension and enrichment curriculum.
Preparation for most of these program units will happen during the allocated Thursday lunchtime study session; however, in the lead up to some associated events additional sessions may be required.
Students will see there are many program units on offer, and due to the busy and already demanding Greenways (year 9 Program) schedule, we recommend that students choose their programs carefully. Many students would like to be involved in everything, but unfortunately this is not possible! Students are not restricted to how many options they select, however due to number restrictions students may not be able to participate in every program selected.
Here is some brief information about each unit:
1. **OzCLO – Linguistics:** The Australian Computational and Linguistics Olympiad is a national competition for year 9 to 12 students. Students will learn strategies to solve fascinating problems in real languages. This unit is especially relevant for students wishing to take English Language in VCE. This competition is on 4 March. https://ozclo.org.au/
2. **Philosophy (Ethics Olympiad):** Students will work in a team of five and prepare using a common series of cases on ethical case studies. Students will also learn some ethical theories to support their views and perspectives. Students will have the opportunity to participate in the Secondary Ethics Olympiad in May or the Middle Years Ethics Olympiad in November.
3. **Hack In A Box – Entrepreneurship Challenge:** Here students will solve a real-world challenge, as provided by a major Australian company such as Village Entertainment. Students will work in a group to find a solution to the problem, and then as a team have the chance to 'pitch' their idea to a Company Executive. During the program, students will be taught a set of innovation tools that have been scientifically proven to boost creative and critical thinking skills. http://www.hackinabox.com.au/
4. **ASX Sharemarket Game:** Working as an individual or in pairs/groups students will receive $50,000 to invest in a virtual sharemarket. In this unit students will develop an understanding of how the sharemarket works and learn how to research companies. Real prize money is awarded. https://www.asx.com.au/education/sharemarket-game.htm

5.	**Year 9/10 Da Vinci Decathlon:** This is a one-day event where in teams of eight students will compete against up to 20 other schools across a variety of academic subjects. A highly energetic and fast paced day. This will require a few additional lunchtime/after-school preparation sessions prior to the competition. http://www.davincidecathlon.com/davinci/index
6.	**Model Solar Vehicle Challenge:** In teams students will build either a model solar car or boat according to specific requirements. Teams will compete at the annual competition held at Scienceworks early in Term 4. https://sites.google.com/view/modelsolar/

Figure 1: Program Units

	Competitions/Advancements
	These competitions or advancements are on offer to Dare2Dream! students; however, they do not require students to attend the Thursday lunchtime sessions. Preparation required is different for each competition.
1.	**CAT Maths Competition:** The Computational and Algorithmic Thinking (CAT) competition is a one-hour problem-solving competition which seeks to identify computer programming potential. No prior experience in computer programming is necessary. The competition is held in April with 6 teaching sessions arranged in the lead up to the competition. https://www.amt.edu.au/cat-competition
2.	**BrainSTEM Innovation Challenge:** Working in teams of four, students will have the chance to work with and be mentored by scientists and academics in the STEM field to design, research and develop a STEM innovation with a real-world application. Visit the BrainSTEM website to find out more specific details about this program. Teams will meet weekly with their university mentor for teaching and support.https://brainstem.org.au/innovation-challenge.html
3.	**Secondary Philosothon:** Mixed with students from years 8 to 11 students will participate in a 'community of inquiry' with students from other schools. This will require a few lunchtime/after-school practice and teaching sessions prior to the competition.
4.	**Tournament of Minds (TOM):** Working in teams of 7, students will prepare for the competition day in term 3. This program requires a high level of commitment but is also highly rewarding. Here students will work to solve a chosen problem, and prepare a presentation where they share their solution to a panel of judges. TOM is highly creative and encourages critical thinking and team work. https://www.tom.edu.au/

5.	**Inter-school Debating:** Here students will have the opportunity to represent their school and participate in a number of inter-school debates.
6.	**Science & Engineering Challenge:** Run by the University of Newcastle, students will be involved in an exhilarating day competing against other schools in fun and engaging, hands-on activities such as designing an earthquake proof tower, building a hovercraft, providing electricity to a city, and creating an environmentally friendly house. This will require a few lunchtime sessions prior to the competition. https://www.newcastle.edu.au/about-uon/governance-and-leadership/faculties-and-schools/faculty-of-engineering-and-built-environment/science-and-engineering-challenge/about-us

Figure 2: Competitions/Advancements

From these offerings in figure 1 and 2, we encourage our secondary students to choose two program units for the year, and two competitions/advancements for the year. However, students can choose four program units, and four competitions/advancements should vacancies exist. They might also choose just one of each, or any combination in between. Our only parameter is that once students commit to a program unit, or a competition/advancement, that they see it through. This provides for a very fluid and flexible program in the secondary school, one that is highly individual and differentiated, but one that can specifically support the student's skill and knowledge development and their aspirations for the future.

Since introducing the four program unit options, and the four competitions/advancements at each year level, we have seen much greater student attendance, significantly more student engagement, and far-reaching rigour when it comes to accepting and working through challenging tasks.

To ensure a focus on learning in such programs, as introduced in the previous chapter, Kanevsky (2017) has created a comprehensive learning specific survey which encourages students to consider their learning both in the planning phase, the progress phase and during the reflective and evaluative phase, but to also consider their learning preferences as part of this process.

In the 2017 book, P*ossibilities for Learning* by Kanevsky, we are presented with the aforementioned student survey which refines the student learning process as a specific and ongoing point of focus. The survey consists of the following learning elements:
- Part 1: Settings for learning
- Part 2: Ideas to learn
- Part 3: Ways to learn
- Part 4: Showing your learning
- Part 5: Lists of possibilities

This exciting survey covers all bases of importance for the student in relation to voice, choice and learning.

YEAR 9 PROGRAM EXPLAINED

In considering the year 9 course I think it is helpful to look at some of the programs on offer and their particular relevance for students at this stage of their development.

The first, the ASX Sharemarket Game is offered as a program unit. In this unit students work in syndicates of one student or more to explore the Australian Stock Exchange (ASX). They learn about sectors including energy, technology, health/medical, financials and so on, and the stocks, or shares of companies available to buy within each. So, for example: Woodside Petroleum in the energy sector, Apple in the technology sector, Ramsey in the health sector, and Westpac in the financials, just to name a few. Students set up their syndicate accounts with a hypothetical $50,000 sum, and over a three-month period learn how to navigate the ASX, investigate stock options, follow stock and sector trends, create watch lists, alert notifications, and buy and sell stocks. They learn the expense of brokerage fees and the ongoing costs of buying and selling. They also learn the value of dividends, these being the share of profits provided by companies to owners of their stocks (shareholders), and they learn how the rate of buying and selling stocks can have a direct impact on stock value as can company successes and setbacks.

Students work through the ASX Sharemarket Game in real time, with real stocks and real values. It is a challenge that is directly linked to the world and what is going on in it. Students can put themselves in the shoes of traders and investors and see what it is like to operate in these roles. They can learn about what works and what doesn't through a realistic life challenge. Many will consequently go on to invest in the stock market in the future with their real earnings. For some, their experience of the game as a student will be their introduction to financial literacy and the strengths and pitfalls of this field. This is real life learning at school. It has purpose and relevance for students and hence in their eyes adds great value to their programs.

The second, the BrainSTEM Innovation Challenge is offered as an advancement. This unit explores an aspect of science, technology, engineering or maths (STEM) of the students' choosing. In this challenge small groups of students think about an investigative focus to which they can make a contribution through research. The group establishes an outline for their task and develops this into a hypothesis, and is then partnered with a doctor or professor in the tertiary sector who acts as the group's mentor. These students with their mentor then work through the research process from initial idea, to aims and purpose, research, literature review, procedure for action, method for implementation, practical action, data collection, data analysis, findings and conclusions. In this work students learn what it is to be a researcher and to bring about action and change through what is tried, tested and learned. These challenges are highly collaborative, encouraging students to rely on one another and their different skills to embrace research most effectively. This gives gifted students an opportunity to gain a feel for what they can do later in their lives while exciting, motivating and engaging them in the rigors of collaborative group research. This can again potentially direct a student's actions for future education and vocational pathways while providing outstanding skill and knowledge development for their current school study.

The third, Tournament of Minds, is offered as a program unit. This unit operates cross-age, involving students from foundation to year 10. In teams of seven, students engage with a creative problem in an area of their choosing: maths, science/engineering, the arts or language/literature. Teams decide collectively on their area of focus and once they have chosen, they engage in a long-term challenge and a spontaneous challenge. In solving the long-term challenge, participants demonstrate their well thought-through solutions by means of a drama conducted in a 4-metre by 4-metre square. This drama involves actors, props and a narrative solution, all developed according to a list of rules or criteria that teams must adhere to. Scores are awarded to each team for their innovation, practicality, creativity and teamwork.

The spontaneous challenge is presented to teams on the spot, at which point teams confer for a short period before creatively presenting a solution back to a panel of judges. Again, the spontaneous problem is subject specific according to the team's chosen focus.

Tournament of Minds brings many challenges but also many rewards. Students work in cross-age groups of seven students. They have choice around the problem that they focus on, and they are presented with challenging, real-life problems which require collaborative problem solving, critical thinking and creativity. Students have a list of criteria that must be met in order to solve the problem, and a designated space in which to solve it. All of these challenges relate directly to life outside the school and the many challenges that individuals and teams will face in the home, at work and in life.

RATIONALE FOR THE PROGRAM

When one considers the rich and diverse nature of these three challenges presented in this year 9 extension and enrichment program, we begin to see the depth, rigour and thought put into the programming, and the practical skills and levels of engagement available to the participants. In sharing just three of the twelve options offered to year 9 students we can see just how exciting school life can be for students.

Why are such programs chosen by gifted students?

We have talked about student voice, student choice, purpose and practicality in terms of skills and knowledge, and preparing students for life outside school in universities and vocational work; but we haven't yet drilled in on key skills.

An advantage of units, competitions and advancements shared through the year 9 examples is that each of the offerings discussed highlights the application of required 21st-century skills. At the World Business Forum in 2017 there was a heavy emphasis on artificial intelligence (AI), and how educators might keep education relevant as technology continues to evolve. Robots can do a lot, and even do much of the work humans have done in the past. Although many algorithms and logarithms can solve basic problems, the human mind has an extraordinary amount to offer above and beyond what AI is capable of. The World Business Forum highlighted a need for educators to continue to hone and develop essential skills. Among these were three of the most critical skills of complex problem solving, critical thinking and creativity (Soffel, 2016).

We desperately need people who can solve complex problems; who can think critically and innovatively about how we see the world and the many issues we face; and people who think outside the box, from different perspectives to generate new and inspiring solutions. We still don't have cures for many diseases, solutions to world poverty, or a streamlined team approach to environmental care. These are some of the biggest problems that are driving our greatest challenges and holding us back in some fields of endeavor. It could be our gifted students who enable the breakthroughs that we so desperately need across the world, and as they become autonomous learners, they want more and more opportunities to develop these skills. The more engaged and inspired they are, the greater our chances are for positive change and extraordinary advancement.

Ultimately what we strive for as educators is to see in our students the very practical nature of application of learned skills. This empowers students to show us what they can do. It demonstrates their skills at work and their mastery, and results in engaged, dynamic and effective learning. Through the Year 9 program I have shared some of the ideas of what has been possible via application of learned skills through the ASX Sharemarket Game, the BrainSTEM Innovation Challenge and Tournament of Minds, but what if students wish to come up with their own ideas and be truly innovative creators of their own destinies?

To be successful in business and in life, students need to have the ability to action their own ideas and starting points, and this should be done for good reasons and with authentic purpose. With this in mind I present Case Study 2, a mini example of what is possible.

MINI CASE STUDY 2 - $20 PROJECT

One idea for demonstrating such action on the part of students has been born from the students themselves. In 2011 I had a small group of students approach me with an idea. The conversation was around using the skills, knowledge and problem-solving abilities attained through the gifted program that had been running in my school. The students felt that it was time for them to give back to the community and be constructive in their future fund raising; to show what they had learned and to display what they could do for the good of others through a very practical demonstration.

The idea was that these students would devise a project, the $20 Project. They would set a list of parameters and criteria for implementation. They would set themselves up in teams of 4 or 5 students, each with a different responsibility, and I would provide each group with a $20 note as a fundraising starting point and one period per week for collaboration and planning. Having a general extension class provision each week made it possible to meet the students' request with some forward planning. Over a period of six months each group would work through a process that enabled that $20 to grow into a much larger sum. The idea was only limited by a team's creativity, their skills and their ability to execute the plan largely in their own time out of school hours. The plan was extensive, there was 'criteria' to meet, duty of care issues to address, ethical challenges to overcome, and all this had to be signed off before the group could start making any money for their cause. In effect, the preliminary administration was a bit like a business plan, so again real-life skills and application at work. The agreement was that the initial $20 start-up amount would be returned to its source (me) at the end of the project, but all profits made would go to a charity of the team's choice. Among the ideas implemented were weekly cake stalls, gardening services, IT support, simple merchandise sales, mother's day and father's day stalls, just to name a few. Each group started very small, making carefully chosen purchases to fuel their projects, then as sales were made the profits were fed back into the business. Students played the roles of director, treasurer, secretary, purchasing and sales, creative ideas and marketing. All assisted at the sales events or in the implementation of the service. At the end of the six-month period there was a final sales event and service day at which point all the profits were brought back to the class and presented via a short presentation on what was done and what was achieved.

LINK TO GIFTED THEORISTS

The $20 Project was so practical in nature it has since highlighted to me a close affiliation with prominent theorist, Robert Sternberg's very practical scientific measures of giftedness and his more recent wisdom addition of active concerned citizenship and ethical leadership (ACCEL), his more refined wisdom model.

Scientific measures of giftedness is shown in that the $20 project business plan sets a prediction about what might be possible by way of experimental action, hence being similar to Sternberg's generating hypothesis, and generating experiments. The $20 Project also required regular review, analysis and editing, or adjustment throughout the project, again all key elements of Sternberg's (2018) scientific measures of giftedness.

However, what really struck a chord for me was the uncanny alignment of the $20 Project with Sternberg's (2017) ACCEL wisdom model. The whole drive behind such a project on the part of the students was based on active concerned citizenship and ethical leadership, a deep desire on the part of gifted people to act on their concerns and demonstrate ethical leadership out of a sense of responsibility. See figure 3 overleaf. The first question that prompted the need for a $20 Project on the part of the students was around answering the questions:

1. How can we make a difference for the good of society using the skills, knowledge and abilities that we have attained?
2. How can we impact the world for good outcomes and demonstrate what we can do at the same time?

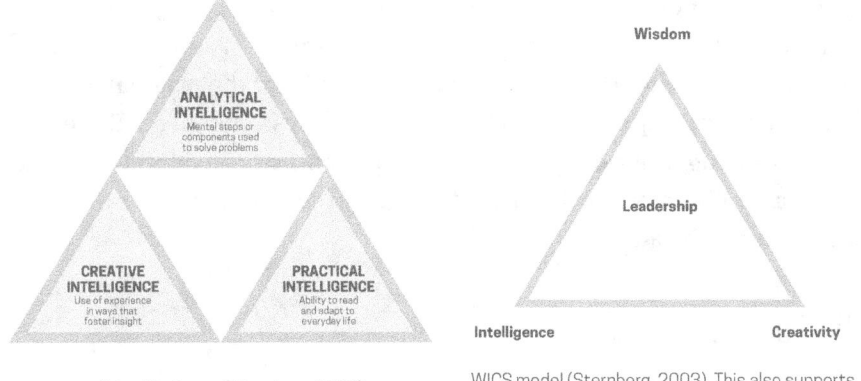

Figure 3: Stenberg's models

When Sternberg grappled with his ACCEL theory in the lead up to its release in 2017, he must have had these types of thoughts in mind. How refreshing it is to see these students aligning in such a practical way, and out of such deep concerns to make a difference.

In the first year of the $20 project implementation, I was moved by the self-initiated process the students had gone through, the way they had worked collaboratively, and their passion, engagement and drive. Observing all of this I was confident that the end product would take care of itself, and sure enough it did with cheques presented at the end of 6 months for over $4,000, $1,500 and a number of sums in between. From a $20 startup, this result was extraordinary and demonstrated in very practical terms just how far these students had come, not just academically, but as concerned citizens.

This work demonstrated to me far more about the students and their learning than any pen and paper test or exam could ever convey, trumping traditional assessment processes tenfold. This work was about life, about being human, being real in the real world, and developing a readiness for life outside school. It demonstrated all of the key 21st-century skills we value. There was creativity through generation of the original idea for the concept, then again in each individual business endeavor. There was critical thinking around duty of care and the ethical considerations, and there was problem solving when working through each point of criteria that needed to be addressed.

CONCLUSION

The future is bright when we consider our resources and increased capability, but with these skills, knowledge and opportunities comes the responsibility to be wise and ethical. Navigating academic pathways and social and emotional health will require good teachers and good decision making. As educators we need to pledge now to use our resources and skills constructively for those whom we reach and impact. When supported and nurtured these students have the potential for exceptional achievements such as critical medical breakthroughs, solutions to engineering problems, creative approaches to environmental care and sustainability, and technological advancement beyond what we thought was possible. We need to be vigilant, aware and responsive to new developments as we empower our students to forge ahead creatively with the greater good in mind.

ACKNOWLEDGEMENT

I would like to acknowledge the insight of Ms Hayley Kuperholz, a former colleague, for her creative contribution to case study 1.

CHAPTER REFERENCES

Fredricks, J., Alfred, Cl, & Eccles, J. (2010) Developing and fostering passion in academic and nonacademic domains. *Gifted Child Quarterly*, 54, 18–30

Kanevsky, L. (2017). *Possibilities for learning survey*. Possibilities for Learning. PFL Survey (possibilitiesforlearning.com)

Soffel, J. (2016). *Ten 21st-century skills every student needs.* World Economic Forum (weforum.org)

Sternberg, R. J. (1997). The triarchic theory of intelligence. In D. P. Flanagan, J. L. Genshaft, & P. L. Harrison (Eds.), *Contemporary intellectual assessment: Theories, tests, and issues* (pp. 92-104). The Guilford Press.

Sternberg, R. J. (2003). WICS: A Model of Leadership in Organizations. *Academy of Management Learning and Education,* 2, 386-401

Sternberg, R. J. (2017). ACCEL: A new Model for Identifying the Gifted. *Roeper Review: A Journal on Gifted Education,* 39(3), 152-169

Sternberg, R. J. (2018). Direct Measurement of Scientific Giftedness. *Roeper Review: A Journal on Gifted Education,* 40(2), 78-85

CHAPTER 4

RE/ENGAGING AND DEVELOPING CREATIVELY GIFTED THINKERS IN MIXED ABILITY CLASSROOMS

AMY HORNEMAN

ILLUSTRATIONS BY SHANIA TAVARGERI

A CREATIVELY GIFTED STUDENT IN HIDING

Meet Vlad. When I first met Vlad, he was a fifteen-year-old student in my English class at my brand new school. In the 'handover' meetings, I was left in no doubt whatsoever as to what kind of ride I was in for with Vlad (for those who have never experienced 'handover', it is a series of lengthy and detailed discussions where we try and prewarn and forearm incoming teachers with insights, wisdom and strategies for coping with the dangers and perils imminent in the upcoming academic year). Imagine if 'handover' meetings were framed as a game of 'I Spy' (you know the one – 'I spy with my little eye something beginning with ...'). Here is how the game would have played out regarding Vlad:

I spy with my little eye something beginning with A...
Answer: Annoying
A: Arrogant
D: Disorganised
D: Disrespectful
H: He-who-NEVER-submits
L: Lazy
R: Rude
S: Sabotaging
T: Troubled
W: Wrecking ball (as in, coming into the classroom and completely wrecking – perhaps decimating is a better word – the entire lesson and possibly the entire year!)

Now it would be nice to tell you that this is one of those 'Hollywood success stories' – the ones where the teacher works alongside the impossibly difficult and troubled student and everything turns around after some climactic potential-disaster-turned-epiphany moment. But I can assure you, this was no 'Hollywood success story'. In fact, every word on that list was accurate and I experienced Vlad in all of his dysfunctional glory in my classroom that year.

In some ways, it would also be nice to think that I'm the only teacher who has ever experienced (and/or survived!) a student like Vlad. But I know that's not the case, and if I had to put money on it, I would bet that you have had to work your way through the messy labyrinth of trying to produce quality learning outcomes from such a student yourself at some stage in your career, and if you're beginning your career, I can absolutely promise that you will!

Here is where it becomes very helpful to become a 'detectorist' (the term coined by the ridiculous but addictive BBC4 comedy of the same name (Crook, 2014) to describe people whose entire life and obsession it is to use metal detectors to look for hidden treasure buried underground): If I'm playing 'I Spy', what is it that I see, and what is it that I'm looking for? Is it possible that when we see a whole lot of surface dirt, grass, sand or rubbish (figuratively speaking), we stop looking there (or we have a classic 'daddy look' and don't look behind or underneath) and miss out on the eureka moments of discovering that there is the potential for some treasure to be uncovered? Is it possible that within each Vlad there is a goldmine of creative giftedness that's never been channelled and developed helpfully and positively? And equally possibly, are there students in our classes who have incredible cognitive and creative ability, but who, for whatever reason, don't get to show us what they know and are capable of? And further still, what about those who do get to show us their creative and cognitive ability? How do we cater for them appropriately so that each student can have the opportunity to learn and grow?

Here are my big questions for this chapter:
What is creative giftedness?
What does/can creative giftedness look like in the classroom?
How can we plan and teach for creative outcomes, thereby bringing out the gold that is present (but sometimes buried – very deeply) within the creatively gifted individual?

WHAT IS CREATIVE GIFTEDNESS?

We all talk about creativity all the time, particularly in educational circles, and for most of my life until several years ago, I had always promoted enthusiastically the absolute certainty that 'I am not creative' because I got the lowest grades ever for art (visual arts) at school – a C grade. It wasn't until a mentor of mine commented on the creativity of my work as a curriculum designer and a teacher that I had to confront this myth within my own understanding: creativity is not necessarily being good at 'the arts,' but rather having the capacity to produce 'something both novel and useful.' This is certainly not limited to our typical classification of 'the arts,' and we will throughout our careers have classrooms full of students who are not only intelligent (that is, they have a high ability for 'catching on,' 'making sense' of things, and 'figuring out' what to do – based on the Cattell-Horn-Carroll theory of intelligence (Carroll, 1993), but who combine a strong intellect with creative giftedness. These individuals have enormous capacity to contribute uniquely to their worlds, which can bring much joy and transformation to the societies in which they live (Sternberg, 2020), but as Steve Jobs (1997) famously reminded us, the creative thinkers, the true innovators of our world are:

> *"the crazy ones, the misfits, the rebels, the troublemakers, the round pegs in the square holes ... the ones who see things differently — they're not fond of rules ... You can quote them, disagree with them, glorify or vilify them, but the only thing you can't do is ignore them because they change things ... they push the human race forward, and while some may see them as the crazy ones, we see genius, because the ones who are crazy enough to think that they can change the world, are the ones who do."*

As with any strength, there is a flipside, which can be difficult to navigate in a classroom (Kim et al., 2013). This next section will explore what creative thinking can look like in the classroom, in both positive and negative ways.

WHAT DOES/CAN CREATIVE GIFTEDNESS LOOK LIKE IN THE CLASSROOM?

Engaged creativity

Creativity in engaged, motivated, conscientious students can be thrilling for both the teacher as well as the student and their peers. E. Paul Torrance (famously nicknamed 'the father of creativity'), a psychologist in the earlier half of the 20th century, devised a series of tests of creative aptitudes, the Torrance Tests of Creative Thinking (1972), which look at the ability of learners to show **originality** (novelty of ideas), **fluency** (number of relevant ideas), **flexibility** (variety of categories of ideas), and **elaboration** (detail expressed in ideas). With this in mind, I bet if you were asked to think of a 'creative' you know who was positively engaged in a classroom, you could describe what their learning looked and sounded like, and your list might possibly look a little like mine:

- The ideas they come up with are completely different to everyone else's in the class (and they are usually very proud of their very quirky ideas!) – **originality**
- It is often difficult to let other students share ideas because this student wants to keep giving their own – **fluency**
- They have a wild sense of humour and playfulness – **originality**
- They get so excited by their ideas they can't help sharing them (either by talking about them boisterously, or by writing them, drawing them or acting them out) and they would prefer to share their own ideas rather than sitting quietly and reading someone else's – **elaboration**
- They make crazy suggestions when trying to solve a problem, bringing ideas from all sorts of places together – **flexibility**
- Creative thinkers who are also artistic show a type of Picasso/Michelangelo/Dali/Monet/Warhol-in-the-making in the margins of their workbooks – **originality**
- They experiment with ideas and objects, sometimes doing unusual things with ideas and objects to reach unusual conclusions or to 're-task' things – **flexibility.**

[Note: if you are interested in actual checklists that have been written to look at characteristics of creatively gifted individuals, look up Renzulli & Hartman's (1971) 'Creativity Characteristics Scale' and EP Torrance's (1969) 'Checklist of Creative Positives']

Mihaly Csikszentmihalyi is looked to as one of the most eminent experts on creativity worldwide, and his theory of 'flow' (1997) has revolutionised our understanding of what engaged creativity looks like (figure 1). Flow, basically put, means the state we get in when the level of challenge we are experiencing matches our ability, particularly in an area of interest. Students in classrooms who are sufficiently interested and motivated, appropriately challenged and adequately capable in a particular area have that magical experience of 'flow'. But unfortunately this state of engaged creative process and production is not the case for many of our creatively gifted students.

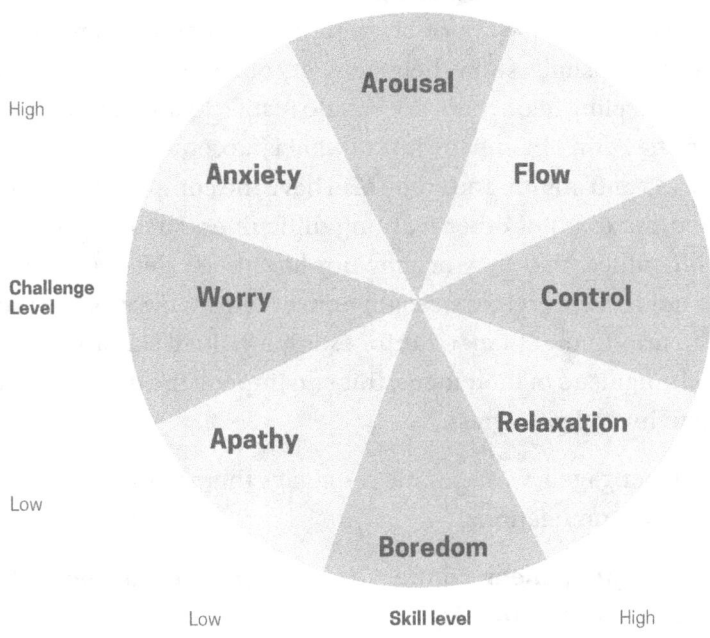

Figure 1: Flow (Csikszentmihalyi, 1997)

Differentiation for gifted students

Disengaged creativity

Whilst engaged, creative thinkers can bring fresh ideas, passion for learning and innovation into a classroom, disengaged creative thinkers can look and sound a lot more like my dear student Vlad from earlier. These students can be the wrecking balls, not only of our carefully and diligently prepared lessons, turning our plans into frustrating, disappointing messes; but they can also be the wrecking balls of their own lives and the societies they live in. As Sylvia Rimm (2019; 2003), an internationally renowned advocate for gifted children and their parents and educators, put it at a conference presentation I once attended, "Creativity is very close to oppositionality: the foundation of creativity is to question, which can get very annoying!"

Creative but disengaged students are often involved in misbehaviour, both within and outside of classrooms, if school restricts creativity and fosters boredom. Regular classrooms can be rigid in terms of how they value and communicate 'acceptable' ways of showing knowledge and creativity. These students then usually show their creativity outside of the classroom but not within it, feeling like school doesn't do justice to their knowledge. In some cases, they don't fit into the box of what is 'acceptable' in terms of showing knowing and ability; and some also have the complicating factor (which is often the case) of other learning difficulties, such as auditory processing difficulties, that may or may not have been detected. These students also might have greater strength nonverbally than verbally (they might prefer to draw rather than write, for example). But if classrooms are entirely verbal-linguistic in their focus, this can impede the display of the student's creativity and giftedness.

If students are disengaged, we can try to re-engage them in two important areas: pedagogical and relational.

Pedagogical – helping them connect (and therefore engage) with school and the school community
- Look for strengths and weaknesses beyond paper testing
- Encourage inquisitiveness, challenging of ideas, collaboration: acknowledge their ideas and use collaborative learning strategies to get students mixing and sharing
- Use creative, real-world, open ended tasks/assessments

- Include hands-on, experiential learning to show practical giftedness and creativity: this is so important in societies such as ours where our education systems have tended to prioritise academic achievement
- Welcome students' knowledge and expertise: reciprocal appreciating

Relational
- Build a positive relationship with students: smile, be approachable, be empathetic
- Be firm but fair: explain boundaries and jointly construct these boundaries
- Encourage inquisitiveness, challenging ideas and independence: don't stamp curiosity out
- Show empathy: validate perspectives
- Seek robust explanations for disengagement and avoid 'lazy' labels

(adapted from Camilleri, 2018; 2017)

There is also a fascinating distinction between conceptual (holistic) and sequential learners (Porter, 2005; 2008): sequential learners tend to learn, as the name suggests, in a sequential way, happy to construct knowledge, skills and outcomes block by block, starting with the basics and and then increasing the complexity. As you can probably agree, most of our classrooms are likely to work in this way, and to prioritise the learning tendencies and strengths of sequential learners. Creative thinkers, more often than not, are conceptual or holistic learners, meaning that they need to work with big picture ideas, and want (or need!) to find their own sequences, patterns or systems of learning within this big picture. These learners often really struggle to learn sequentially, and therefore are less likely to show their giftedness; this can lead to a teacher misunderstanding a student's capability, as our testing tools don't let them show what they're good at (we're holding the wrong hoop for them to jump through). This highlights the idea that we are often looking for something different to what we are getting (remember our game of 'I Spy' from earlier).

Ultimately, if we want our students to learn in our classrooms, and if we want our gifted students to have the opportunity to learn and grow at a rate that suits their needs and abilities, we need to ensure that they are engaged in the learning. And there are certainly ways we can plan for engaging learning.

HOW CAN WE PLAN AND TEACH FOR CREATIVE OUTCOMES?

When dealing with creatively gifted students, we need to make sure that we don't simply look at creative output (talented outcomes) of students and ignore the creative potential (giftedness) that our students might have. We need to plan for, and implement, teaching and learning experiences that will allow creative potential to be developed and expressed.

The Maker model (1982) is the most widely accepted and referenced model for differentiating instruction, regardless of a student's individual needs or ability profile, and this model provides an extremely useful framework for looking at how to engage creatively gifted thinkers in our mixed ability classrooms. This model was also discussed in Chapter 2 – see pages 42–44. I am going to use Maker's four categories of Content, Process, Product and Environment to provide some ideas and strategies. This of course is not a comprehensive guide, but rather a list of ideas and considerations that I know can make a difference to how well creatively gifted students engage with the learning environments we create.

Figure 2: Maker model of curriculum differentiation

QUADRANT I: CONTENT

Content refers to what we teach: the material we plan for and actually cover in our curriculum.

Teaching up

Teaching up (Tomlinson, 2021; Sousa & Tomlinson, 2018) means starting with a rich and powerful curriculum for all learners that challenges advanced learners, and supporting students as needed to engage with the curriculum and to succeed. Part of teaching up obviously involves content and ideas, as well as the need for working primarily with higher order thinking skills (endearingly called HOTS in the vernacular), using taxonomies such as Bloom's famous one and focussing on analysis, evaluation and creating.

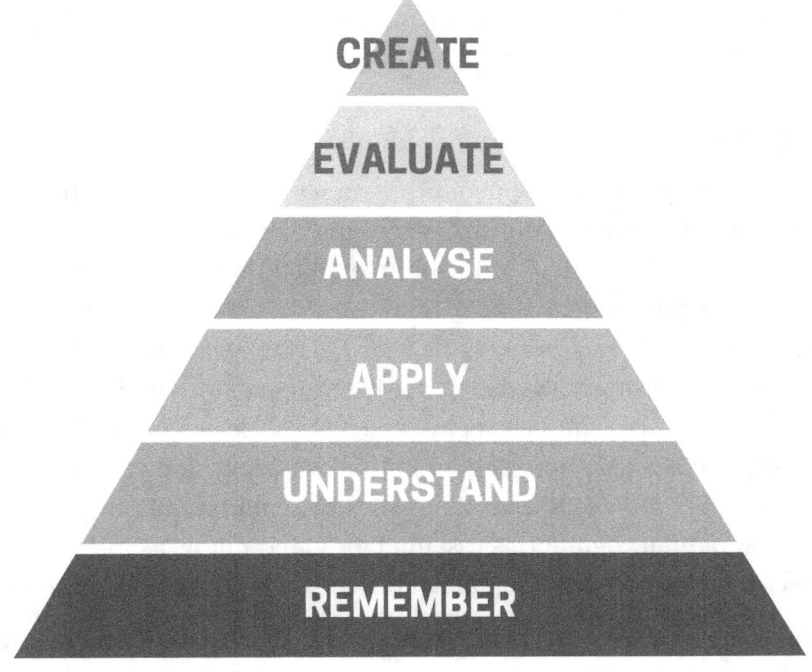

Figure 3: Bloom's taxonomy

The idea of teaching up creates space and opportunity for creative thinkers to play with big, rich ideas and for curiosity to run free. So often our curriculum is designed to teach to the middle or to ensure that learners who struggle will cope with the content on offer. But teaching up allows the most creative minds to have the opportunity to climb up a learning ladder of disillusionment and challenge before they reach the excitement and satisfaction of new learning: James Nottingham (2017) developed the idea of the Learning Pit as a means of showing the process and importance of learning pits. Through having to climb their way up and out of the 'learning pit', creatively gifted students have to build the intellectual and creative muscles required to innovate and create meaningfully, as well as to meet challenge with growth and resilience, rather than choosing the path of least resistance. This also allows creative thinkers the opportunity to explore their own definitions of failure and success in terms of learning, which enables development of a **growth mindset** (Dweck, 2008) and **grit** (Duckworth, 2016), terms which have become so important in the social and emotional development of gifted individuals.

Thinking tools and strategies

While teaching up is a slightly more abstract way of thinking about the content we plan, a more concrete suggestion is to explicitly teach creative thinking tools and strategies. This is an excellent way to engage creative thinkers in a metacognitive way: when you start speaking their language, they're in! Tony Ryan's *Thinker's Keys for Kids* (1990) is a set of 20 critical and creative thinking tools which, used in sequence and embedded within curriculum design, can be taught explicitly as metacognitive learning. Students are not only being asked to think critically and creatively, but they are made aware of what they are doing and naming the process: this level of metacognition is essential for gifted minds as they learn to consciously train and develop their creative and critical thinking skills.

We mentioned Torrance and his Tests of Creative Thinking (1972) earlier; like Ryan's thinkers keys, these tests and the skills they focus on, can actually be taught explicitly and used within curriculum processes as a way of helping students engage their creative thinking brains. Not only are these tools explicitly focused on identifying, training and developing creative thinking, they are also an enormously entertaining pedagogical tool. The absolute magic lies in the ability these tools have to tap into the goldmine of a creatively gifted thinker's brain. If you have a disengaged student who you can see has a creative streak, try some of these tools and see what comes out in your classroom! Even better, give the students some options for creative thinking tests and tools, and see which ones they go for ... then ask them why.

Choice

Much work has been done on the power of allowing students free choice to follow an area of passion or interest (eg Reis, 2018; Roberts & Boggess, 2016); who knows where this passion or interest could take a student in the future? Csikszentmihalyi's (1990) flow theory, as mentioned earlier, is a defining work in this area, and important to consider when deciding what content we will teach. If we allow students to sometimes make choices about what content they will delve into, we might find that a whole lot of engagement and creative production goes on (Glasser, 1999). When students follow their interests, when they are provided with sufficient challenge, and when they have the skills and ability to follow it though, the essential elements of creating the flow state are achieved.

QUADRANT 2: PROCESS

Process refers to how we go about teaching and how students go about learning (and hopefully vice versa!).

Allowing for flow

If we can somehow manage to set our classrooms up as learning environments where students are given the opportunity to reach a 'flow state', then they can experience:
- Complete concentration on the task
- Clarity of goals and reward in mind and immediate feedback
- Transformation of time (speeding up/slowing down)
- Intrinsic reward in the process
- Effortlessness and ease

- Balance between challenge and skills
- A space where actions and awareness are merged, thereby losing self-conscious rumination
- A feeling of control over the task

Part of enabling this flow state is allowing students some element of choice over how they go about completing tasks (Im & Varma, 2018). Open-ended tasks can be very good for this: allow students to decide on what they are doing and how they are going to get there, and allow conceptual or holistic learners to show how they would set up and see through solutions to problems or innovate to come up with new ways of doing things. The outcome of flow is true creativity: individuals make contributions to learning and producing that are truly original as well as useful.

A dialogic approach

> *"I cannot teach anybody anything. I can only make them think".*
> *"Wonder is the beginning of wisdom."*
> *"Strong minds discuss ideas, average minds discuss events, weak minds discuss people."*

Socrates, 5th century BC philosopher, is famous for his pedagogy of questioning. By why is questioning so powerful? What is it that questions achieve that other forms of pedagogy lack? Questions guide our thinking and point us to deeper ways of knowing and understanding, and they help us share our learning journeys. For teachers, questions and the resulting answers show us how and what students think and know (Dillon, 2004). Teachers can actually differentiate their curriculum by asking, responding to and following on from questions between teachers and students as a conversation between minds (dialogic teaching), rather than one expert (the teacher) talking and the novices (the students) listening (didactic teaching) (Munro, 2020; 2013).

Usually our gifted creatives are the ones who ask the most difficult, perplexing, out-there and sometimes confronting questions. This can make some teachers nervous. I can sense some questions bubbling: Doesn't this give too much control or power over to the students? Doesn't this leave me open to my classroom and the lesson turning into 'feeding time at the zoo'?

Shouldn't I decide what the students need to learn and how they should learn it?

If we think of teaching like playing in a jazz ensemble, it might help clarify the power of this type of teaching for creative thinkers: in jazz, there is an underlying structure, guide and framework of a tune played in a certain key, based on and reliant upon certain technical and scalic skills and knowledge; the musicians then build upon these essential elements to create their own contributions which fit into the existing structures and which bounce off each other's contributions as a dynamic process of collaborative music making. This is called improvisation, and I would argue that improvisation in our own classrooms is essential if we are to effectively engage with our creative thinkers: we need to allow room for creative input and output to breathe. We also need to be able to use existing teaching and learning structures and frameworks to allow ourselves, as well as our students, the freedom to explore, to improve, to bounce off one another, and hopefully to delve into new territory.

I think if I had shied away from dialogic teaching with my student Vlad, there would have been absolutely no success at all in engaging that creatively gifted thinker, as he would have felt that his contributions were not welcome and not valuable. I also know that Vlad loved to share his ideas with me and to use me as his intellectual sparring partner. Denying him this opportunity to share and to spar and to challenge through questioning and discussion would not only have led to some rather unpleasant outcomes for me and for his class, but even more tragically, he would not have learned and grown in my classes.

QUADRANT 3: PRODUCT

Product refers to the outcome of student learning: what they produce as a result of their learning (usually but not always assessment tasks).

Low floor, no ceiling (LFNC) or low floor, high ceiling

As a general guide for differentiated learning, when we design and implement learning experiences, we should create space both for students who struggle conceptually (low floor) to have somewhere to land their thinking and learning (making a start), as well as those students who are highly creative and far more advanced conceptually to have a chance to find a space where they can still learn (high or no ceiling), and can still get stuck in a problem that they need to find their way out of, using HOTS and complex problem solving skills. Papert (1993, 1980), who coined the LFNC idea, said, "The role of the teacher is to create the conditions for invention rather than provide ready-made knowledge" and to provide them with "tools to think with over a lifetime", rather than limiting how high and far the creativity process can take the student. Another way of thinking about this could be to ensure that you are climbing as high up on thinking taxonomies (Bloom's (Anderson et al., 2001), for example – see figure 3) as possible, and allowing students to do as much of the 'creating' level as they can; this allows curiosity to take its own path and allows us to see where students can take it: we might be surprised by what they come up with when we give them opportunity to show us what they can do!

An example could be a unit on water pollution, where the task asks students to build a certain type of water filter. A LFNC adaptation of this task could be giving students the option of designing and building their own solution to water pollution, according to certain criteria (functionality, usability, innovativeness etc). Or in mathematics, a task that asks students to solve a particular mathematical problem could be adapted to a LFNC option: write your own mathematical problem on a certain topic or focusing on a certain set of skills, and give a few different solutions. Adapting the tasks (products) that the students are being assigned can be a simple yet effective way of giving creatively gifted students the opportunity to show where their creativity could take the task, which could lead them to innovating for the future!

Problem-based learning and performance tasks

Real-world, open-ended, authentic tasks, such as performance (or GRASPS) tasks (as part of the understanding by design (UBD) method of curriculum design (Wiggins & McTighe (2005)), can be practical tools for assessment tasks that can help take the ceiling off for creative learners. These tasks insist on real world audiences, authentic role taking, design thinking processes, and using HOTS for most of what they are required to do. The power however lies in the choice students are empowered to make about what their product will look like and what process they go on to solve an authentic problem in an authentic way.

A sample performance (GRASPS) task proposed by Wiggins and McTighe (2005) is:

G – Goal: The goal (within the scenario) is to minimise costs for shipping bulk quantities of M&Ms.

R – Role: You are an engineer in the packaging department of the M&M Candy Company.

A – Audience: The target audience is non-engineer company executives.

S – Situation: You need to convince penny-pinching company officers that your container design will provide cost-effective use of the given materials, maximise shipping volume of bulk quantities of M&Ms, and be safe to transport.

P – Product/performance and purpose: You need to design a shipping container from given materials for the safe and cost-effective shipping of the M&Ms. Then you will prepare a written proposal in which you include a diagram and show mathematically how your container design provides effective use of the given materials and maximises the shipping volume of the M&Ms.

S – Standards and criteria for success: Your container proposal should provide cost-effective use of the given materials; maximise shipping volume of bulk quantities of M&Ms; be safe to transport. Your models must make the mathematical case.

Other such learning opportunities that involve students in solving problems creatively, such as Tournament of Minds (TOM), future problem solving (FPS) and creative problem solving (CPS), rely on creative thinking and on the HOTS found in thinking taxonomies to be successful (Merrotsy, 2018). Criteria for such competitive learning opportunities often contain words such as: creative strength, fluency, flexibility, elaboration, originality, lateral thinking, and research applied. These types of competitive opportunities can be very effective in engaging creatively gifted students in the urgency and relevance of utilising their creative cognitive strengths to improve their worlds.

Choice of product

Choice is always going to be a winner for creatively gifted students, as discussed above. Choice of product is just as important as choice of content and process. If we insist in every classroom for every subject that students come up with products that we have pre-determined, and we assess and grade them according to our pre-determined markers of 'success', are we ever leaving room for them to truly innovate? Could we see our classrooms as training grounds for our future innovators and those who are going to gift our society with breakthrough technologies or ideas? If so, we might need to let go of the reins of 'product' and allow our students to show us what they are capable of. This could mean that some students might design their own scientific experiments; some students might create working models or original inventions; some students may create a sculpture, a dance or a ballad rather than writing an essay each time for each subject, following the same rigorous routines and pre-determined patterns. The sky is the limit when it comes to how students could show what they know and what they are capable of creating. Perhaps a conversation with individual students can be a very useful starting point in giving choice of product?

QUADRANT 4: ENVIRONMENT

Environment refers to the dynamic (physical, intrapersonal and interpersonal) that we set up in our classrooms and in our interactions with our students.

The physical and aesthetic environment of our classrooms

The typical understanding of creativity being confined to the creative arts, while not helpful in engaging creative thinkers outside of the creative arts domains, can give us clues as to what is characteristically creative about theses domains, and how we can apply some of this to our own classrooms, regardless of the subject/s we teach. Creating learning environments that allow students to tap into and derive inspiration from aspects of the creative arts can be enormously powerful in engaging creative thinkers; ideas include: playing music while students brainstorm or are involved in heavy cognitive activity; allowing students to express their ideas through art, dance, drama and music; and using visual brainstorming and thinking routines that involve colour, shape and other visual elements. We also need to recognise the value of allowing creative thought and exploration time to breathe: do we ever have time to let ideas germinate and grow, and to create a physical space that could be conducive to the flow state?

Our personality and interpersonal dynamic as teachers

In conjunction with the physical space, the interpersonal space we create can provide optimal learning experiences for our creative learners. 'Openness to experience' as part of the big 5 personality theory (Costa & McCrae, 1999) has been described as being the highest predictor of creative potential. If we ourselves as teachers are able to be open to experiences within our own learning environments, this creates a path for engagement with learning, and allows for a shared celebration of creativity, rather than shutting down or 'squashing' creative thinkers and their contributions (which may or may not be what we are used to or within our comfort zone, particularly if we do not perceive ourselves as being highly creative individuals ourselves!). If we create learning environments that are safe spaces for students to have new experiences, to play with ideas, to allow their curiosity to explore and expand, for their creative and intellectual appetites to be fed, we may find that the learning is richer for all involved, including ourselves!

Taking seriously the contributions of our students is a key that I have found to be invaluable in my teaching, particularly with students like Vlad. Some students make contributions in class discussions which on the surface seem to be provocative, seeking a negative reaction; but being open to our students' creativity can allow us as teachers to see our students as incredible goldmines of knowledge and creative potential. Are we ever intimidated by how much our students know or can do, or by where their creativity takes them in terms of creative process or production? If we are open to experience, and if we are creating learning environments with no ceilings, we should have an expectation that some of our students will far surpass our own knowledge and ability niveaux, and this should not only be OK with us – this should be a marker of our success as teachers of these highly creative individuals!

Relationship and rapport with our students

Any student who gets the vibe from their teacher that 'I see you and am trying to understanding you' is going to respond positively. I know for Vlad this was certainly one of the biggest factors in successfully building a positive and effective learning relationship. If we can build relationships with our students that make them feel like they belong and are known by us, and like we can all enjoy the space that we inhabit together with them, they are far more likely to learn and engage effectively.

In maximising creative potential within gifted student populations, two key ideas are worth prioritising: knowing and counselling students and seeing self-actualisation as a shared journey. We cannot underestimate the role we as teachers play in going on that journey with our students, rather than leaving them to their own devices to try and work it out on their own. One-on-one mentoring is a very powerful way to get to know students, to find out about their interests, passions, fears and dreams. Students need adults who will see them, know them and mentor them through the challenges. We can help by being willing to walk the journey with them through the process of developing their gifts so that they can feel the satisfaction that comes from truly being understood and making the contribution to the world they were born to make (Kerr, 1999; 1996).

What we look for and how we engage with what we experience

Going back to our game of 'I Spy' with Vlad, could it be possible that we as teachers could reinterpret behaviour (while – critically – still holding them accountable for unacceptable behaviour)? When reflecting on my experiences with him, these are the subconscious psychological conversions I made:

A: Annoying = **Bored** – "Please tell me something I don't already know".

A: Arrogant = **Frustrated** – "I actually know a lot and have so many creative ideas but I would love to be able to share them. Ask me and I'll tell you what I know and how my wildly creative brain sees the world".

D: Disorganised = **Not easily programmed by the teaching** – "I don't think/work like that so I find it hard to tick your boxes. I'd like to try a different way of doing what you're wanting."

D: Disrespectful = **Feeling disrespected** – "The bar is too low, the ceiling is too low and this whole building stinks".

H: He-who-NEVER-submits = **Perfectionism** – "What if it's not good enough? Then I'll look like an idiot and I know I'm not".

L: Lazy = **Disinterested and demotivated** – "Why should I bother? Give me something new to learn and to sink my teeth into. Let me loose with some creative licence and I'll show you someone in flow".

R: Rude = **Desperate** – "Please see who I am and what I'm capable of, and take me seriously as a creator and as someone who has something novel and useful to contribute to the world [but I'm afraid that will never happen]".

S: Sabotaging = **Hungry** – "Give me some intellectual food of substance and depth. Engage my brain and allow me the space to work out what I might like to do creatively in response to substantial and deep ideas".

T: Troubled = **Troubled** (spot on!) – "I can't make sense of the world; I haven't had the perfect life for whatever reason; I'm struggling and I make poor choices; it doesn't mean I don't have anything worthwhile to say or contribute – help me understand who I am and the contributions I could make".

W: Wrecking ball = **We can work with this** – Let's find a way to respectfully learn together [you're not allowed to wreck the learning for others so I will hold you accountable for your behaviour; but I'm not going to interpret your struggles or your contributions as a wrecking ball for my lesson].

CONCLUSION

So what's the end of the story of Vlad? I actually honestly don't know, but the story hasn't finished yet for him. What I do know is that our classes provided a rich and stimulating environment for him (as well as for me!) to learn in, and that he was able to show an incredibly creative intellect through our classroom discussions and through a collaborative study of the literature our course covered.

Ask yourself the same questions I do: What can I do in my classroom to help engage creative thinkers, and to possibly reengage creative thinkers who have somehow decided it's too hard or too boring to participate fully and positively? How can I look at ways of setting up learning spaces and planning for learning opportunities that foster expression and exploration of creativity through (among many, many others):

- Content: Teaching up, thinking skills, choice
- Process: Allowing for flow, dialogic approaches
- Product: Low Floor No Ceiling, open-ended performance tasks, choice
- Environment: Physical space, personality and openness as teachers, rapport and relationship building?

Perhaps you have a Vlad in your class right now. Or perhaps you have had one in the past. Remember: there is gold in every student, and just maybe the creative thinkers - who may well cause you the most grief and may make your teaching the most challenging – have a lot to say and a lot to contribute, and they may just need a hole that's slightly rounder to 'fit into' so that they can bring the gift of their creativity to their world!

CHAPTER REFERENCES

Anderson, L.W., Krathwohl, D.R., Bloom, B.S., & Bloom, B.S. (2001). *A taxonomy for learning, teaching, and assessing: a revision of Bloom's taxonomy of educational objectives.* Editors, Lorin W. Anderson, David Krathwohl; contributors, Peter W. Airasian et al. (Complete ed.). Longman

Camilleri, D. (2018, March). At Risk of Disengagement. In S. Nikakis (Chair), *Gifted Twilight Sessions.* Conference conducted at Xavier College, Melbourne

Camilleri, D. (2017, July). Creative Thinking in Regular Classrooms. In J.L. Roberts (Chair), *World Council for Gifted and Talented Children Biennial Conference.* Conference conducted at UNSW, Sydney

Carroll, J.B. (1993). *Human Cognitive Abilities: a survey of factor analytic studies.* Cambridge University Press

Costa, P. & McCrae, R.R. (1999). A five-factor theory of personality. *The Five-Factor Model of Personality: Theoretical Perspectives,* 2, 51–87

Crook, M. (Director & Producer). (2014). *Detectorists* [Television series]. BBC Four

Csikszentmihalyi, M. (1997). *Finding Flow: The Psychology of Engagement with Everyday Life* (1st ed.). New York: Basic Books

Dillon, J.T. (2004). *Questioning and Teaching: A Manual of Practice*. Wipf and Stock Publishers

Duckworth, A. (2016). *Grit: The power of passion and perseverance*. Toronto, Ontario, Canada: Harper Collins Publishers

Dweck, C.S. (2008). *Mindset: The new psychology of success*. New York: Ballantine Books

Glasser, W. (1999). *Choice Theory*. New York: Harper Perennial

Im, S. & Varma, S. (2018). Distorted Time Perception during Flow as Revealed by an Attention-Demanding Cognitive Task, *Creativity Research Journal*, 30:3, 295–304, DOI: 10.1080/10400419.2018.1488346

Jobs, S. (1997). *Apple – Think Different* [Video]. YouTube. https://www.youtube.com/watch?v=YBJAvi3A0H8

Kerr, B. (1999). *A Handbook for Counselling the Gifted and Talented*. Melbourne: Hawker Brownlow Education

Kerr, B. (1996) Is Self-Actualization Optional? in Kerr, B. (1996) *Smart Girls Two – A New Psychology of Girls, Women and Giftedness*. Melbourne: Hawker Brownlow Education

Kim, K. H., J. C. Kaufman, J. Baer & B. Sriraman (Eds.). (2013). *Creatively Gifted Students are not like Other Gifted Students: Research, Theory, and Practice*, 69–88

Maker, C. J. (1982). *Teaching models in the education of the gifted*. Austin, TX: Pro-Ed

Merrotsy, P (2018). Creativity and Giftedness. In Jl Jolly & JM Jarvis (Eds) *Exploring Gifted Education: Australian and New Zealand Perspectives*. Abingdon, Oxfordshire: Routledge

Munro, J. (Speaker). (2020). The Research Files Episode 56: John Munro on gifted education [Audio podcast]. *Teacher Magazine*, ACER. https://soundcloud.com/teacher-acer

Munro, J. (2013). Teaching gifted students: A knowing and thinking-based framework for differentiation. *CSE Seminar Series Paper 225*. Jolimont, Vic: Centre for Strategic Education. http://www.cse.edu.au/content/teachinggifted-students-knowing-and-thinking-based-framework-differentiation#sthash.88uWDabj.dpuf

Nottingham, J. A. (2017). *The Learning Challenge: How to Guide Your Students Through the Learning Pit*. Thousand Oaks, CA: Corwin

Papert, S. (1993). *The children's machine: Rethinking schools in the age of the computer*. New York, NY: Basic Books

Papert, S. (1980). *Mindstorms: Children, Computers, and Powerful Ideas*. New York, NY: Basic Books

Porter, L. (2008). *Gifted children: Meeting their needs* [Video recording]. Adelaide: Small Poppies International

Porter, L. (2005). *Gifted Young Children: A guide for teachers and parents* (2nd Ed). Australia: Allen & Unwin

Reis, S. (2018). Survival Secrets on the Role of Passion in Talent Development. In Roberts, J.L. & Boggess, J.R. (2016). *Teacher's Survival Guide: Gifted Education.* Melbourne: Hawker Brownlow Education

Renzulli, J.S. & Hartman, R.K. (1971). Scale for rating behavioural characteristics of superior students. *Exceptional Children*, 38: 243-248

Rimm, S. (2019, July). The Paradox of Creativity and Rigour. In J.L. Roberts (Chair), *World Council for Gifted and Talented Children Biennial Conference.* Conference conducted at Nashville, TN

Rimm, S. (2003). Marching to the Beat of a Different Drummer: The delicate balance between creativity and oppositionality. *On Raising Kids.* 14:2.

Roberts, J.L. & Boggess, J.R. (2016). *Teacher's Survival Guide: Gifted Education.* Melbourne: Hawker Brownlow Education

Ryan, T. (1990). *Thinker Keys For Kids.* South Coast Education Region, Queensland: Tony Ryan

Sousa, D.A. & Tomlinson, C.A. (2018). *Differentiation and the Brain: How neuroscience support the learner-friendly classroom.* (2nd Ed.). Melbourne: Hawker Brownlow Education

Sternberg, R.J. (2020). Transformational Giftedness: Rethinking Our Paradigm for Gifted Education, *Roeper Review,* 42:4, 230-240, DOI: 10.1080/02783193.2020.1815266

Tomlinson, C.A. (2021). *So Each May Soar: The principles and practices of learner-centred classrooms.* Alexandra, Virginia: ASCD

Torrance, E.P. (1972). Predictive Validity of the Torrance Tests of Creative Thinking. *Journal of Creative Behaviour*, 6:4, 236-262

Torrance, E.P. (1969). Creative positives of disadvantaged children and youth. *Gifted Child Quarterly*, 13, 71-81

Wiggins, G. and McTighe, J. (2005). *Understanding By Design.* Association for Supervision and Curriculum Development (ASCD)

CHAPTER 5

PROVIDING SCHOOL TRANSITIONS FOR GIFTED AND TALENTED STUDENTS

CARMEL MEEHAN

Awareness without action is worthless!
– Phil McGraw

CLASS TO CLASS/SCHOOL TO SCHOOL

Awareness is the key ingredient in transitional success. If you believe that you have a heightened awareness level then please teach it and if you have not then please learn how to acquire it, prior to commencing the tasks involved in transitioning a child who possesses heightened academic abilities.

Identifying and responding to each student's individual learning needs can be complicated and also rewarding. It is vitally important to acknowledge that there are at least three parties involved in the learning of gifted students – the student, their parents and their teachers past and present.

The privilege of being charged with the task of transitioning gifted and talented students may lead to many growth producing relationships with some of the most interesting, challenging and inspiring students that you will be fortunate enough to encounter in your years as an educator. However, the challenge is to ensure that the transition process is as seamless as possible.

Certainly, they present as challenging, inquisitive and lateral thinkers, often described as being tricky students who possess a very high intelligence quotient. These students can show teachers how to be a co-learner and enjoy the challenge of learning how to laugh and enquire, and to feel and learn both deeply and laterally. They are complex people!

Many arrive at their new educational setting feeling anxious and experiencing feelings of fear and nervousness. Acknowledging and honouring these fears can change a student and teacher association in a positive way.

By working together with a receptive teacher, new students are able to move onwards and upwards in terms of being a team of two or more co-students.

As a bonus they also understand 'corny' jokes and fire better ones back at the teachers which is quite a powerful co-learning tool. I would suggest that teaching the gifted and talented students is an honour, a cross and a privilege, however they also make teaching a joy and an educational journey.

EFFECTIVE TRANSITION REQUIRES HEIGHTENED AWARENESSES!

Positive introductions

Prior to accepting the enrolment of a gifted student, it is critical that the school staff understands giftedness and has a shared awareness about what it means for the learning culture of the school to cater for students who will require curriculum stretch.

The school staff would be wise to audit its curriculum definitions, processes, protocols and beliefs so that they all become pro-active in embedding the new student support awarenesses.

Every child will experience anxiety and worry to a lesser or greater degree depending on individual temperament and the degree to which the child is familiar with the culture and climate of the new school or class. Therefore, one of the basic challenges faced by teachers is to ensure that all students are given positive and exciting introductions at the commencement of each term or year.

The transition processes and procedures employed by teachers whose task it is to ensure student transition is as seamless as possible, need to work with a certain degree of flexibility and heightened awareness. For example, shared information between schools, parents and the students should be ongoing prior to and after the enrolment is accepted by the new school. This can be by informal meetings or by more formal meetings, tests and responses to programme outcomes.

The importance of this transition suite of acts and structures cannot be too greatly emphasised because they are critical in forming students' attitudes and feelings about their new way of being a successful student. Some schools baulk at using the label 'gifted and talented' however if we understand this label fully, we will know that we are not only speaking of the student's academic ability but also about his or her holistic suite of characteristics – social, emotional and academic, including learning abilities and disabilities.

The learning behaviours of gifted and talented students require a sound understanding by their teachers about the student's learning history, strengths and weaknesses in addition to their personal ambitions and passions.

Is transitioning a gifted and talented student any different to a common transitional process?

Examining the desired requirements for the seamless transition of a gifted and talented student requires some informed thought and preparation coupled with professional learning about giftedness. It would be very helpful for the new school or class to have relevant information passed on to them about how and why they consider the student to be operating in the gifted domain for example, what were their identification procedures and provisions?

For teachers who are charged with the task of successfully transitioning a gifted and talented student it is critical that they know how to identify the strengths and behaviours of gifted students and to be aware of what is current thinking and learning about scaffolding their success in terms of being a confident and competent student.

Selecting the most effective transition co-ordinator

There are many great teachers in our schools, but some seem to be able to brilliantly and quickly form a productive and growth producing relationship with a transitioning student. They appear to effortlessly be flexible in their dealings with new students, possess a warm sense of humour together with a heightened awareness and sensitivity to the needs of others. These are the characteristics that stand out as being desirable in a transition co-ordinator.

Essential professional learning for a gifted and talented coordinator would include a clear understanding about asynchrony of gifts, and/or talents, and in the areas of physical and emotional development. The intensity of these elements in the gifted and talented student or adult's persona needs to be fully appreciated by all school staff but initially by the transition co-ordinator.

For transitional teachers of gifted and talented students, not only will there be issues of academic placement but concomitant with giftedness usually comes heightened intensity of feelings and emotions and sometimes awarenesses and feelings of social inadequacy. It matters that it matters for the gifted person and it is worth remembering that the parents of gifted students are often gifted themselves and have a very important role in the transition process.

Social and emotional awareness

It is essential that gifted and talented student's emotional triggers be known and understood by the transitional co-ordinator and that they be passed on to all the other staff members as soon as possible in order to circumvent any possible emotional 'melt downs' by the student.

Experienced teachers, parents and educational experts strongly believe that the underlying factor that should guide all aspects of transition is extreme awareness.

Examples would be an awareness of the student as a developing young person, the many facets of life that define his or her place in the societal group at the time of transition and the multiple positive or negative aspects that are part of the student's everyday life. By this I mean personal history in terms of schooling, family circumstances, cultural norms and temperament.

Level placement?

It is very helpful for class placement of the gifted and talented student that they bring to the new school or class a profile of them as a learner, either a portfolio of prior work, evidence of prior levels of achievement individual learning plans plus any social and emotional issues that the student may be struggling with, now or in the past.

According to research undertaken by Peters (2019) and others, up to 10% of students perform four or more grade standards above the standards used in regular classrooms. Therefore, the challenge for educators supporting the transition of students into a new school or class is to know what level they are operating at and to cater for them appropriately.

Who are the gifted students?

Linda Kreger Silverman (2002), in *Upside Down Brilliance* very clearly states that parents are excellent identifiers of giftedness in their children: 84% of the children whose parents say that they fit 3/4 of the following characteristics, listed below, score at least 120 IQ (the superior range). Over 95% show giftedness in at least one area, but are asynchronous in their (uneven) score and that their development and their weaknesses depress their IQ.

It therefore stands to reason that the professionals such as child psychologists, doctors, social workers, parents or caregivers of the student should be involved in any school's transitional procedures to some extent depending on the age of the child and its personal circumstances.

The characteristics listed by Silverman are as follows:
- Reasons well
- Learns rapidly
- Has extreme vocabulary
- Has an excellent memory
- Has a long attention span (if interested)
- Sensitive (feelings hurt easily)
- Shows compassion
- Perfectionism
- Intense
- Morally sensitive
- Has strong curiosity
- Perseverant in their interests
- Has high degree of energy
- Prefers older companions or adults
- Has a wide range of interests
- Has a great sense of humour
- Early or avid reader (if too young to read, loves being read to)
- Concerned with justice, fairness
- Judgement mature for age at times
- Is a keen observer
- Has a vivid imagination
- Is highly creative
- Tends to question authority
- Has facility with numbers
- Good at jigsaw puzzles.

Knowledge of these characteristics and what they may look like are critical for all teachers who are charged with transitioning students so that they can facilitate a smooth entry into a new class or school.

A critical element of the transition process is that a teacher's awareness level needs to be heightened and broadened (hopefully by study and experience) and that they be sensitive to the possibility of the student experiencing a heightened fear, nervousness and worry about their transition coupled with the physical symptoms of sleep impairment.

It is of course quite natural for a student to be anxious about the new learning environment and as a consequence the initial contact with the school may be flawed and will require an ongoing connection between the transitioning teacher and the gifted and talented student in terms of informal and formal meetings and interactions. For example, in areas such as sport, art, chess club, and library.

Actions

Kesner (2005) in his research work at Georgia State University states 'an effective teacher must recognise the gifted child's unique abilities and needs and provide the appropriate curricula challenges along with the appropriate affective environment'. Kesner's challenge for all teachers then is to streamline the transtion of their students in the affective domains, in particular, those who also have been identified as having an advanced ability in one or more curriculum areas.

Suggested aims would be that:
- Growth producing relationships between teachers and students need to be developed as soon as possible, so that the student knows that she or he is actually seen and understood by the teachers.
- The student needs to have some input in developing a individual learning plan at the new educational setting and be aware that ongoing review and assessment are the responsibility of all stakeholders.
- Teachers of gifted and talented students undertake professional learning to better identify and understand behaviours exhibited by these students.
- Many practicing teachers need to complete extra studies and professional reading about the ways to best cater for the gifted and talented students from transition until graduation and are therefore able to recognise disruptive and spaced out behaviour for what it actually is, namely bored.
- Shared understandings, practices and learning behaviours across the school need to give life to the school's belief that they will meet the cognitive and affective academic needs of each individual student.

Logistics

There are many practical measures that can be undertaken by school staffs to ensure that gifted and talented students and their peers are confident and comfortable in their new school setting.

Simple physical expectations, for example, using the lockers and coping with the behaviours of other students in the locker rooms plus temperamental locking devices may result in high levels of anxiety and angst, this is because the time taken to perform this seemingly simple task has flowed on to embarrassments and late arrivals in classes.

For many students this is a small incident in a very busy day, however because of a heightened awareness and sense of anxiety often part and parcel of being gifted, in addition to a desire to keep a low profile and to be seen as almost a perfect student, then using the locker room is fraught with danger. One student said it was so stressful for her that she now carries all her school supplies to each lesson. As yet, she was to find a teacher that she could discuss this matter with, as growth producing teacher/student interaction was for her a work in progress. Sadly, she had approached a teacher about this challenge, but he seemed to find it a very trivial matter and failed to see her genuine distress.

Effective teachers of the gifted need to motivate, inspire, reduce anxiety and understand their high levels of sensitivity.

Balanced curriculum topics

Some students interviewed about their personal transitioning experiences reported that they were not receiving a balance of positive and negative topics in subjects and said that their teachers were all asking them to learn about things that were preceived to be about killing the plant and/or threatening their future.

While they all agreed that these were topics that they needed to learn more about, they believed that a steady diet of gloom and doom across the prescribed curriculum was keeping them awake at night and interfering with their need to be emotionally balanced and have some optimism in their learning.

The message here is for school staff to examine the content they teach across the curriculum and to ensure there is a balance between troubling subjects such as wars, environmental challenges and earth keeping and contrast them with some more positive subjects, possibly with English and humanities where the prescribed curriculum would provide some relief from all the negativity of other subjects.

WHAT TEACHERS NEED TO UNDERSTAND ABOUT THEIR GIFTED AND TALENTED STUDENTS

Asynchronous Development

Students who have a high ability in some academic areas may not have a similar ability level in all curriculum areas.

A well concealed disability may be hard to recognise and can be cleverly compensated for by a smart student. Teachers need to be aware that a concealed disability may be in the physical, academic, mental, social or emotional domains.

It is advantageous to assume nothing about a student and to broadly and deeply test, so that a well-structured learning plan can be drawn up, the results of which will allow the student to build on all levels of curriculum to effectively support their learning journey.

It is a very wise move at transition to test all students in all subjects as soon as possible, if they have not already been assesses using a raft of authentic ability tests.

Most gifted and talented students have asynchronous development and their self-knowledge can cause then much distress and embarrassment amongst their peers. Extreme care needs to be taken in all school timetabling to ensure that the gifted and talented student knows the expectations imposed by the school rules and protocols and can manage the logistics and expectations of the new school or classes. There will be some students who for various reasons are only partially enrolled at a school. For example, they may be receiving social, emotional or physical support at settings outside the school precinct. For example; they may be studying at a different campus because the subjects they are taking are not offered at the school, or they may be receiving treatment at a particular clinic that is supporting their growth and development.

Some schools employ a student 'buddy' system to assist new and partially enrolled students to become aware of the student culture and understandings about a new school or class and also inform them about what transpired at the school in their absence.

Building a working relationship with the student

It is the teachers' job to ensure that a positive working relationship is developed between both parties. Pastoral care, an awareness of the extremes of sensitivity that may be a part of the student's persona, background knowledge and awareness of what the student brings with them, need to be discussed and understood.

Students arrive at the school with different ways of knowing and thinking which they will draw from and cross reference with their life experiences and their cultural backgrounds. While exceptions in the degree of sensitivity may be due to a 'quirky' and sensitive genetic makeup, for most they are able to gain sufficient confidence to become successful students.

To examine these perceptions and identify both their gifts and weaknesses the teacher would be wise to apply some scaffolding, such as some mentor and monitoring meetings between the student and appropriate staff members so that the student has a point of reference where he/she knows that no question is too trivial and confidentiality will be honoured.

The need to timetable more structured meetings with G&T students as soon as possible (preferably on day one of the new school year or prior to that date) is critical, so that the social, emotional, physical and academic health of the student is supported.

Identifying key factors

Some gifted and talented students welcome an opportunity to display their gifts and talents while some are reluctant to do so and others totally 'fly under the radar', preferring to conform and not draw attention to themselves at all.

When endeavouring to discover the gifts and talents of a transitioning student it is imperative that the teacher does his or her homework and finds out all that is known, recorded and anecdotally told to them about this student. Knowledge means having the power to become an effective mentor!

It is important to the transition of gifted and talented students that the student believes that the teacher knows who the student is and what are his/her passions and that some can be shared and discussed. Thus, a relationship is formed and some genuine teaching and learning can follow the relationship and be remembered and sustained. An example of this would be to know what goes on in the student's life outside of school and making casual enquiries and comments is one method of building a mutual understanding about some of the holistic perceptions of the student's life.

It matters that it matters!

Orientation variables

Transitional changes for the student may be physical, social, emotional and cultural. The size of the school can be a huge change and quite overwhelming if the transitioning student has come from a smaller school to a larger school, therefore physical orientation is essential, especially for visual learners.

Issues of identity need to be addressed. For example; a high ability student in a small school can have a profile of success but the same student, upon entering a larger school, may find that they lose some of their identity and expectations of their place in the academic pecking order. Their identity as they knew it has been lost.

Some student orientation props could be a clear and concise school map (an essential tool hopefully colour coded), a clear and well-structured time table and a hard copy diary.

Time tabling, mapping and time trailling exercises can make the transition so much more comfortable for the student. If possible, students new to the school need to walk around the school and get a feel for the logistics before all the other students arrive onto the campus.

Imposter syndrome

Some students do not believe that they have the potential to succeed at a very high level and tell themselves that they have just been lucky in the past to score well, and that sooner or later they will be unmasked as imposters. Such students can flourish in a well scaffolded school environment and their transitional class placement needs to be well researched and documented. One-on-one sessions with a school counsellor may need to be arranged to support the student's self-esteem and to adjust their self-talk.

Past experiences of bullying

If the student has experienced bullying at their previous school or class the fear, apprehension and 'flight or fight' mentality will be lurking in the back of his or her mind. The new school would again be wise to alert the school counsellor to this prior experience and begin a scaffolding action to allow the new student to feel empowered to deal with this counterproductive behaviour towards them going forward. I find the following quote attributed to Brewer (2015) very helpful, when supporting and creating positive self-talk: "Bullying is a horrible thing. It sticks with you forever, it poisons you. BUT ONLY IF YOU LET IT."

Peer pressure (Forced choice dilemma)

Gifted and talented students who dumb down their ability levels to fit in with the 'in crowd' are quite sure that this is the best approach to peer acceptance; mainly because for most students there is an under lying need to be liked and feel that they are socially acceptable. Many gifted and talented students will be reluctant to show their knowledge and skills in front of their peers and risk being singled out as different and nerdy. Bullying past experiences can also motivate gifted and talented students to lie low in terms of showing their superior knowledge and skills in a new learning environment. The challenge for the student's transition into a new setting is to place them with like-minded peers who will support their giftedness and/or talents and possibly become their co-learning friends in and out of the school setting.

Jung, McCormick & Gross (2018) have written some very interesting and informative papers dealing with the forced choice that is faced by gifted and talented students i.e. their dilemma being whether to be true to themselves and reveal their gifts and talents and consequently risk ostracisation by the 'socially in group' of students, or alternatively to be true to their gifts and talents and risk exclusion from the social groups. Effective transition will be able to scaffold a student making a choice to be true to themselves.

Transitional teachers need to be prepared to meet students who choose to undersell their abilities. Many gifted and talented students will strongly state at the onset of their transition that for them, standing out as gifted and drawing attention to themselves as being a very advanced student is not a transition option. Developing a close relationship with such a student would be a very wise move and may ultimately build the confidence needed to stand alone as a gifted and talented student.

Interestingly, if the academically gifted student is also physically gifted, they are usually socially accepted and can show their giftedness across all curriculum areas.

E. E. Cummings, believes that "the hardest challenge is to be yourself in a world that wants to make you someone different" (2016). However tangible supports for developing self-confidence and positive self-talk are mentors and teachers who believe in their gifted and talented students and are willing to stand by them through the tough times and the triumphs.

Spiritual intelligence

Adolescent students tend to question, dissect and push family or societal boundaries that have previously guided their moral compass.

Many families live their lives by trying to abide by strict traditional or religious beliefs, therefore transition teachers and other staff members need to be aware of the ways that these family/sociatal beliefs may be challenged and discussed within the comparatively safe school setting. For many, however, variations in religious or societal beliefs are a taboo discussion at home.

Small children seem to be more in touch with their spiritual selves than adolescents and accept without question a spiritual and imaginative world. However, as students mature, they question most rules and regulations that have been decreed by adults and religious beliefs are no exceptions.

Spiritual guidance and in-depth discussions about comparing religions; genders and earth keeping beliefs are a healthy intellectual development as students examine the world into which they were born.

Teachers need to be aware of individual family and cultural taboo subjects and understand that some parents and religious leaders frown upon such conversations and try to force their beliefs on others rather than allowing questioning, discussion and debate to proceed.

This approach is unlikely to be meekly accepted by a gifted and talented student who usually possesses a very high level of understanding in areas of physics, mathematics and science etc.

In a Catholic school this can be a great debate and should be encouraged, but based on authentic texts and research familiar to all parties.

It is quite possible that when a close relationship is formed with the transition teacher the student may start the debate within the safe confines of the mutual respect each has for the other.

An effective action would be for the teacher to ask to include significant others in the discussion, for example the school chaplain so that the discussion is based on sound understandings which underpin the modus operandi of the school.

Hygiene awareness for teenagers

Due to puberty, bodily changes and personal cleanliness concerns during adolescence, it is wise to be aware of the school's protocols when a student is needed medical or hygiene assistance or advice at their new school.

It would be helpful to assume nothing about the transitioning student's bathroom routines and for teachers to present some sessions with students who are at or, on the brink of puberty, explaining the ways that their bodies are changing and developing. With the onset of puberty significant bodily changes are taking place and students need to be made aware that bodily cleanliness is essential.

Teachers can significantly assist teenagers to create cleanliness routines that ensure that they are caring for themselves and others that they come in contact with, especially focusing on armpits, genital areas, hair and feet.

Student group interaction will occur on a regular basis and it is an unselfish act by the transitioning teachers to ensure that the students are not creating 'off putting' odours which stand in the way of their acceptance into the class group.

For some students this can be a budget issue as well as a steep learning curve, therefore a wise teacher will surreptitiously assist them to purchase the required cleanliness products and if necessary, demonstrate their functions. Students who are new to the country may not understand where and how to obtain the necessary products and a buying excursion may need to be organised.

Student leadership options

Some students come to the new educational setting having been in leadership positions at their previous schools. Some may aspire to continue to put their hand up to be a potential leader but others want to step back from taking on leadership and responsibilities in the new school setting. Teachers should check out how the student views leadership and whether it is something he/she might wish to pursue going forward. In discussion with primary school student leaders entering secondary school, I heard that most would accept leadership positions if voted in further down the track by fellow students who actually knew them to be honest and reliable students, rather being chosen by staff members based on transition information.

Acceleration and justice

Most gifted and talented students have some degree of asynchronous development and their class placement may need to be closely considered, including acceleration by subject or class level. Decisions need be made that meet the social, emotional and academic needs of the student, coupled with how the acceleration will be scaffolded at the school.

Many teachers are reluctant to support student acceleration for fear of social and emotional repercussions for the student however, for many G&T students who are operating well above the class norm, it gives them the academic stretch to indulge their love of learning and engage in more meaningful conversations with peers and teachers.

Often it is their teachers who need to understand more about filling any educational gaps the student may have and help the student to adjust to his or her new way of being, an engaged learner. The transition co-ordinator may need to become the mentoring and scaffolding support person for the teachers involved in the acceleration exercise in order to keep the needs of the child central in all that occurs.

Transition awarenesses audit for reflection and discussion

- Can I/we identify the learning profiles of all the transitioning students?
- Are all learning profiles catered for at this school?
- What are the behaviours a teacher may observe in transition meetings and teaching groups that may indicate a student is possibly gifted?
- Are students with disabilities having their gifts and talents catered for?
- Does my curriculum stretch the student's ability while supporting the disability?
- Does the level of student support alleviate stress and anxiety for the student and class teachers? How will that happen for the student in the transitional phase of their education at my school?
- The aim of all transition should be to effectively and efficiently manage change and to support and get to know the student so that a working relationship can be formed between them and the teachers. How is this occurring at your school?

- Are transition meetings including the school counsellor, the care givers and other support personnel ongoing, therapeutic and informative for all concerned?
- What measures could teachers employ to identify gifted and talented students' transitional requirements in the areas of academic, social and emotional wellbeing?
- Are new students to this school or class (who seem to have transitioned effectively) being supported by committed mentors who developed a growth producing, ongoing relationship with them?
- What research and professional learning will I need to undertake to add to my understanding about gifted students and adults?

CHAPTER REFERENCES

Brewer, H. (2015). *The Cemetery Boys*, HarperCollins

Cummings, E. E. (2016). E. E. Cummings: Complete Poems, 1904–1962. Liveright

Jung, J. Y., McCormick, J., & Gross, M.U.M. (2012). The forced choice dilemma: A model incorporating idiocentric/allocentric cultural orientation. Gifted Child Quarterly, 56, 15–24

Kesner, J. E. (2005). Gifted Children's Relationships with Teachers. *International Education Journal*, 6(2), 218-223

Peters, S. J. (2022). The challenges of achieving equity within public school gifted and talented programs. *Gifted Child Quarterly*, 66(2), 82–94

Silverman, L. (2002). Upside-Down Brilliance: The Visual-Spatial Learner

Silverman, L. (2007). Perfectionism: The Crucible of Giftedness. *Gifted Education International*, 23(3), 233-245. https://doi.org/10.1177/026142940702300304

Weyns, T., Colpin, H. and Verschueren, K. (2021). The role of school-based relationships for school well-being: How different are high- and average-ability students?. British Journal of Educational Psychology, 91: 1127–1145 e12409. https://doi.org/10.1111/bjep.12409

CHAPTER 6

PROGRAMS AND PROGRAMMING IN SECONDARY SCHOOLS

GERALDINE NICHOLAS

A HOW-TO FOR NOVICE TEACHERS

Welcome to the world of gifted education or as it should be known – education for the gifted (Dettmer, 1985). If you are reading this, it is because you are interested in meeting the needs of your high ability students; or you have noticed the ability of some of your students far exceeds the capability of others in your classes; or you are in charge of the gifted and talented program in your school or, best of all , you are just keen to learn more.

Whichever is your scenario, the world of education for the gifted is one of many possibilities. There is no one model or rule of best practice. What is necessary is what is best for your context and your students. You will do endless research and reading. You will follow certain scholars and models.

You will learn and try to implement some suggestions Let me assure you that to do something is always far better than to do nothing.

As I write this chapter, we are in the world of Covid-19. Covid-19 has brought to the world of education a new way of doing that is unprecedented. It is both exciting and somewhat scary to see and imagine the possibilities of delivering learning and teaching. The time presents a chance to imagine differently the delivery of knowledge and skills. We have a chance to modify the learning and teaching to better meet the needs of our students. Technology presents unlimited options as we teach and interact via a multitude of platforms. We can use technology to meet the zone of proximal development of every student; to challenge them; to make them feel just a little bit uncomfortable as they learn; for the student to say "I am not there yet". We can design activities, learning sequences and opportunities that set up success as essential and then ask questions to assess themselves within the learning pit (Nottingham, 2017). We can diagnose their knowledge and then set up summative and formative feedback that is "timely, appropriate and learner-focused" (Crockett and Churches, 2017).

SEEKING A DEFINITION

Alright, enough about dreaming and scheming and let's get back to how and what of programs and programming for gifted students.

Let's start at the beginning – a definition. The hardest thing about gifted education is the lack of agreement surrounding the exact definition of the term 'gifted'.

The 2000 Macquarie Dictionary states gifted as an adjective meaning "endowed with natural gifts, talented". The noun *gift* is the "ability or special ability". Interestingly most scholars recognise it as ability, generally above their peers. Not everyone agrees that giftedness is a measure of IQ. Most see giftedness as a characteristic based upon behaviour, learning and performance. Whatever the definition, most agree that a gifted child has potential and generally requires academic challenge (Coleangelo, 2010). However, a definition that only recognises academic ability can ignore those of practical intelligence or even emotional and spiritual intelligence. The definition needs to be broad and encompassing.

Most scholars differ on what percentage of the population could be given the gifted label. Gagné states 10% and as most Australian states use Gagné's DMGT 2.0 (Gagné, 2009) model to develop and inform their gifted program, the value of 10% shall stay within this discussion. Irrespective of how many are needing the label within a population, overwhelmingly, there is evidence that such a cohort needs to reflect the constitution of the wider population beyond the school gates. So, within every school, the gifted and talented community should be able to find within it representatives of the various ethnic and socioeconomic groups. Gifted kids, no matter what their cultural background, should be able to see themselves within the cohort at your school.

Students who do not consistently achieve high academic results and those with learning difficulties (twice exceptional or 2e) should also be found within the cohort. These underachieving and 2e students are often overlooked. 'Normal' standardised testing regimes such as ACER PAT (Australian Council of Educational Research Progressive Achievement Tests) tests and the National Assessment Program – Literacy and Numeracy (NAPLAN) do not pick them up whereas ACER Abstract and Reasoning testing and Cognitive Abilities Test (CogAT) can recognise the students who have a different way of being gifted. To find the gifted child, you must know more. There are a multitude of excellent articles, chapters and scholars (Silverman, 2013) that can detail how to identify and how to cater for the needs of these exceptional and different children.

The lack of a definition will always be a quandary when looking at how to educate the gifted. However, what is important to educators who are practising in the field, are the characteristics they display. Worrell et al (Worrell et al., 2019) define being gifted as exhibiting superior performance in a domain when compared to their peers. Gagné sees the word 'gifts' as having a biological basis, an innate and informal natural ability or an aptitude, that with deliberate practice, shows itself in an adult with talent or outstanding mastery in their chosen field or domain. The adult has developed or achieved competencies that are above 90% of the population. This is easily seen in the world of sport or art where so many children show potential but without the right environment, intrinsic motivation or opportunities, only a few display and achieve mastery above and beyond their peers.

DEVELOPING A PROGRAM

Finding a definition is important as this will inform and guide the practice by which our gifted children are educated. Previously, many scholars referred to programs by which we do 'gifted education'. The move to transfer the thinking to the development of talent has merit as a point of view. Gifted education should be as regarded as education for the gifted as it is a developmental process where talent and potential are recognised and encouraged.

Setting up a program is not easy. There are too many possibilities, too many models, too much advice. Confusion can reign and thus a program could appear not to meet the needs of the cohort it is meant to serve.

Personally, the definition of gifted determines the program. The program needs to reflect how such a cohort is seen within a school. For many, education for the gifted, means a protocol that allows for advanced academics. Thus the program needs to recognise students who have been identified as having performed in a field/s above their peers and are now in need of development and advancement.

THE ADVENTURE BEGINS ...

The how-to program needs to start with an identification process. Most scholars (Rogers 2002, Renzulli and Reis 2014) agree that using IQ as the sole value for identification is dangerous as it does not easily recognise those who do not test well in a standardised format. Such tests are informative but a variety of methodologies is best. Multitude measures should include teacher references such as Renzulli's Scales for Identification of Gifted Students (SIGS), student questionnaires, parent surveys, anecdotal evidence and even participation certificates in programs such International Competitions and Assessments for Schools (ICAS) competitions and science talent search as well as leadership citations. Level of achievement in some activities should not form the only basis of selection. Participation allows the selection agent to see where a child's interests and abilities lie and such information can assist with differentiation of curriculum.

Achievement data from sources such as ACER can be useful when comparisons with years above and below are made. If possible, when testing, students who continually achieve within in the ninth or eighth stanine, should be encouraged to undertake tests at least one year above their level. Take for example, a student who is in year 7 or 12/13 years old and undertakes the ACER PAT maths test. The score when compared to other year 6s is within the 99th percentile. The data is further compared to year 7s – 99th percentile and year 8s – 98th percentile. What does the data tell? For this student, when compared to 98% of the fellow year 8 or, 14 years old, he/she still outshines them.

Yet another student undertakes the same tests but as a year 8. Achievement data shows that when compared to the year 9 or 15 year old cohort, this student outperforms 99% of both year levels as a year 8 student! Ideally this student should be allowed to undertake year 11 (or VCE) mathematics as a year 9 student. However, sadly not too many schools are equipped or willing to allow the subject acceleration to occur. School based restrictions means that such a capable student is unable to progress into higher level studies until at least year 10. For this child, their progression has been placed into a holding pattern. If you are lucky, the child is happy to maintain their studies within the confines of the current curriculum structure. However, there is always the threat that such a child will seek placement within another school that encourages subject acceleration resulting in the loss of such talent. Or in a worse case scenario, the child will be in a holding pattern of talent development and if you are lucky, they will ride it out. If you are unlucky, the child could act out or become an underachiever. Wasted talent development is not a place we want any child to experience.

How do schools respond to the above quandary? For many students, schools focus on the right hand side of the bell curve (see Chapter 1, page 20) with well-established and rigorous programs and this means that gifted individuals miss out on the development of their talent. Some school possess a pull out program, some have a well thought and resourced differentiation program and some have a dedicated cohort of students of high ability.

For the students cited above, they could be placed within a defined and long term program for the education of gifted students. For such a program, students could be selected based on an application process such Renzulli's scales for identification of gifted students (SIGS) that uses a rating scheme for a multitude of characteristics as well as parental information and teacher reference. Selection is achieved using the conversions of the ratings into scores. A cut off needs to be established and 80% is a suitably high mark.

Figure 1 (adapted from Rogers, 2017) is an example of the profiles that can be used to select candidates for a program. Teachers are asked to indicate how frequently a trait is observed and ideally a selection of attributes including motivation, creativity, leadership and subject specific qualities should be included.

Learning Characteristic	4 Consistently	3	2	1 Rarely
Has unusually advanced vocabulary for age, uses terms meaningfully				
Has quick mastery – usually requires 1 or 2 repeats				
Has quick recall of factual information				
Wants to know how and why of things				
Is a keen and alert observer				
Read a great deal on his/her own, often prefers material beyond their current age level				

Has large storehouse of various topics; often beyond interests of age peers				
Has rapid insight into cause-effect relationships				

Figure 1: Sample survey questions (adapted from Rogers, 2017).

The scoring regime is based upon Renzulli's scales for identification of gifted students (SIGS) or Rogers (figure 2) so that a score is established for each trait. By averaging the scores, a total score is achieved and with a final 'cut off' level established, decisions as to possible candidates can be determined. A worthy post note is that entrance into such a program should be monitored throughout the year. Teacher recommendations and anecdotes, parental discussions and the child's opinions should be noted. Academic achievement must also be monitored as there will always be children who deserve to enter. If there is any sign of struggle, recommendations can be made for the student to exit. There should also be a 'no shame' policy as being asked to move out or requesting to do so, if not a sign of failure. In this case, the program did not fit the child.

Student	High achievement	Leadership	Academic	Arts	Under-acheivement
A	4	3.4	3.8	3.2	1
B	2.3	3	2.25	3	3
C	4	4	4	4	1

Figure 2: Sample of categories for consideration into gifted program. Adapted from Renzulli's SIGS.

Establishing a cut off score of around 80% allows those who sit below the top ten percent to be included. It allows for those who have great potential to benefit from inclusion in the program and thus receive a rigorous and advanced curriculum. It provides an opportunity to learn beyond what many may have experienced in the past.

The program needs to be built around a cohort of students experiencing an accelerated content of the year above. Ideally the student should be able to enter the subject of greatest strength, interest or readiness. Another possibility is to accelerate into core subjects – maths, English science and humanities either as whole group or as a combination of at least two. In this exemplar, the curriculum could be compacted so that students enjoy a faster pace of learning. Added to this is the ideal of doing 3 years' worth of study in two years or even 18 months. The model needs to be reflective of the needs and demands of the school. Ultimately, the vision and mission of how a school sees the place of the gifted and talented program needs to drive both the selection of students and the protocols of the service program.

A program of acceleration has huge academic benefits for the student beyond just academic achievement. The social and emotional advantage of finding 'like-minded' peers means that some finally find their tribe. For others, they have always seen themselves as awkward; as the one who does not fit or who sees no one else like them. Here finally, they find people who possess qualities like they have, who laughs at the same jokes or who has the same intense interests. Other advantages include a higher achievement level as the students often push each other. For each of these students their needs are met.

Part of the success of the program is the level of content expertise teaching staff possess. The staff need to have taught across all secondary levels, they must be passionate about their learning area as they need to know content, understand the learning and scaffolding necessary. They should be able to develop and use a variety of resources and strategies that encourage high academic achievement. They should understand and know the scope and sequence of skills and knowledge that these students need to know and do as well as those that are 'nice' to know and do. In addition to content specific knowledge, staff need to have a good grasp of what a student within the program looks like, in other words, what characteristic (Silverman, 2013) they possess. Staff should also move out of the program once they have taught within it after three years. This ensures that more staff get to experience the joy and complexity of teaching and learning the high ability students requires. Moving staff on a regular basis can help prevent the complacency (and perhaps laziness!) of designing and using innovative ways of learning when you are too comfortable within a particular program.

PROGRAMMING … MEETING THEIR NEEDS

Once determination of what the gifted child looks like within your context has been decided, the 'what' of programming needs to be addressed. Programming is essentially the provision of learning experiences and opportunities in all their different formats. For the novice, this process of seeking the best program is complicated by a huge array of possibilities. The aim is not to cover all that is possible but to consider a few in depth leaving further exploration to occur at your leisure.

For the sake, of argument, the following will be considered:
- Integrated curriculum model (ICM) by VanTassel-Baska and Little
- School enrichment model (SEM) by Renzulli and Reis

Whatever the model, the following questions need to be considered:
- Is the program driven by theory?
- Does the program have a strong research base?
- Is the program easy to implement and understand?
- Is the program flexible and adaptable?

As Renzulli (Renzulli, 2001; Renzulli, 2012) reminds us, the label 'gifted' should be attached with the aim of developing high potential in the top 20% of our student population. Renzulli also reminds us to look for not only intellectual traits and behaviours but to recognise the non-intellectual traits as well.

Before we venture on the path of well-developed models of programming, it is worthwhile pausing to consider the comparative benefits, or otherwise, of some delivery options.

a. **Integrated classroom support**

   Here the regular classroom teacher is present. High end challenges (Tomlinson, 2009) can be provided. Often the teacher is left to design the program, produce resources and can have little knowledge or training in what a gifted program needs. It can be viewed as a band-aid method of delivery. It can be seen as an 'extra' for staff and students and may not build upon general classroom knowledge. Furthermore, students identified for inclusion, can be solely based on Maths and Reading achievement scores like ACER PAT test, NAPLAN or on demand testing. Despite the many obvious problems such a program possesses, as pointed out by Schroth (Schroth, 2013) it is far better to provide something that to do nothing.

b. **Cluster grouping**

   This is where gifted students are placed with other gifted students within a class. This model allows for the development of a curriculum that is faster in pace and deeper in knowledge. It is beneficial as students work at their own pace and within their own instructional level. Gaps in knowledge can be addressed quickly and students can indulge in products of learning to meet their level of interest and readiness. Such a provision allows for the gathering of like-minded peers and social emotional support. For some of these students this may be the first time they feel comfortable in the class.

c. **Pull out programs**

   In this option, students are withdrawn from their regular classroom and work with a specialist gifted teacher. The program may be one specifically developed in a subject of choice such as mathematics. There is opportunity to build on their preferred area of interest and knowledge and to extend into the curriculum that is above their peers. For example, year 8 maths students may be extended using instruction from year 9 or above depending on the ability of the student. Again, for these students, the potential for social emotional support in being with like-minded peers of similar or higher ability brings pleasure in being challenged and able to explore content in detail and with extended time.

d. **Special classes**

   In this case either enriched or accelerated content is provided, usually out of school hours. Examples are programs held over the weekend or school holidays such as GATEWAYS or the University of Melbourne extension program where high achieving students can study university level subjects in their final year of school. GATEWAYS comes at cost to parents.

e. **Select entry schools**

   These public schools are dedicated to the education of gifted students. The SEAL program in Victoria (Select Entry Acceleration Learning) refers to either a whole school or a program offered within a school. SEAL schools can offer specific strategies usually in the academic arena though some offer sport as well as music. Entry can be via entrance exams. Victoria has four dedicated SEAL schools in which high performance results need to be maintained as well as participation in extra-curricular activities.

f. **Acceleration**

   This service delivery is a form of educational intervention in which progress is through an education program at rates faster than the pace or level above that is typical of their age (Colangelo et al., 2004). As explained comprehensively in *Nation Deceived* (Colangelo et al., 2004) there are 17 different forms of acceleration. For some students, their understanding may be up to 18 months above their peers, thus there are a variety of options available.

   - Year level acceleration is advancement into at least the year above. This may be a wholesale proposition so that the child is able to undertake all subjects from the year above.
   - Subject acceleration is content based acceleration. Students are placed with older peers in their area of advanced ability so a year 7 student may be placed into a year 9 English class. Careful and considered timetabling and communication is needed for this to occur. There is also the need for that student to not have to undertake or make up for learning that has been missed due their presence in their accelerated class.

g. **Curriculum compacting**

As the name suggests, this is the compacting or reduction of basic learning activities. Time is gained and should be used for advanced content instruction or in participation in enrichment activities such as Science Talent Search or Tournament of Minds. Here pre-assessment is important in informing the exact level of mastery that the student possesses and thus planning to meet their level, need and interests and extending them beyond.

h. **Telescoping**

This delivery method is where instruction is covered in less time than is typical of the age or year level. The end result is general advanced grade or year level placement and thus content and knowledge.

SPECIALIST WAYS OF DOING

The section above discussed generic methods of educating the gifted. There is a plethora of services that are bound by research, driven by theory, easy to follow and flexible. The following will be considered:
- Integrated curriculum model (ICM)
- School enrichment model (SEM)

ICM is an approach developed by Joyce VanTassel-Baska. The model has emphasis on content that is advanced, utilises higher order thinking and learning that is cross disciplinary and concept based. Products of learning are generally based on research, inquiry skills and inter-connected across disciplines. For example, students may investigate what may happen if bee populations continue to decline or what strategies can be used to win or solve a puzzle. ICM allows for the design of differentiated curriculum that provides "experiences that are sufficiently different from the norm to specialised intervention" (VanTassel-Baska and Little, 2017). VanTassel-Baska states that the use of a trained educator of the gifted is essential as is "appropriate instructional and assessment procedures" so that student learning is maximised. Furthermore, she asks that when designing curriculum, teachers define what is important for the student to know and be able to do at their stage of development. This is an important consideration as advancement into content and skills of the year/s above is not possible if the student has gaps and misconceptions that do not allow for deep understanding. The curriculum for the education of the gifted should be exemplary. It should be based on the habits of experts in the field. It should be relevant so that real world issues, problems and solutions are explored. Acknowledgement is made here that gifted students desire depth and complexity and that the products of learning need to include creativity and collaboration as they should be encouraged to display their learning in formats that reflect the knowledge and skills of practising professionals. For example, science or experimental lab reports should include details of hypothesis, data presentation, discussion and conclusion that supports the hypothesis to explain; uses data to explain trends as well as looking at areas of improvement. Language should show understanding of scientific concepts as well as the protocols of scientific report writing. The lack of literacy and accuracy is no excuse in poor scientific writing as being able to convey and communicate scientific ideas is a key component of experts in the field.

The use of content standards such as those from the Australian Curriculum is a further viable method of generating projects that can assess learning. Choice in the product is essential for the gifted child as it allows them to display through a medium that allows exploration and feels comfortable for htem.

The use of differentiated content is an important consideration when developing programming options. Renzulli's School Enrichment Model (SEM) presents another way. He reminds us to drive the desire to bring about change in a school by examining the "meaning and purpose" (Renzulli and Reis, 2014) of the plan. SEM like ICM is a theoretical model that guides the process of learning, informs curriculum content and assessment as well as the instructional strategies used. SEM has been developed over many decades and has been scrutinised through detailed research. Renzulli sees this as a way in which talent can be developed whilst providing opportunities so that the function of the delivery service is to provide for the education of the gifted.

SEM's major component consists of:
- Systematic and ongoing assessment of students' strengths.
- Provision of "enrichment opportunities, resources and services" (Renzulli and Reis 2014) that allow for the development of strength.
- A flexible approach to both the differentiation of curriculum and school time.
- Development of the professionalism of staff so that they become leaders in curriculum, staff development and learning as well as program planning.
- Creating a diverse learning community that reflects the diversity of the school community.
- Implementing a culture of collaboration amongst the entire school community.

SEM, like so many approaches developed to educate the gifted, can be applied so that the general school population can also benefit. SEM is made up of three essential components:
- School delivery
- Resources
- Organisation.

a. Service delivery

Teachers need to understand who their students are. Identification data consisting of strengths, abilities, interest and learning profiles are as important as well as periodic review and analysis of the data. Doing this, allows for decisions regarding enrichment experiences in and out of the classroom to be investigated as well as a search for acceleration opportunities which would enhance and inform career aspirations.

Besides identification, techniques for curriculum modification and differentiation must be explored. Such techniques include curriculum compacting, opportunities to display mastery in subject/s of interest as well as instructional strategies that allow students to use their time more productively and in a more challenging way.

b. **Resources**

    A well-stocked, up-to-date and divergent supply of resources is essential. Current thinking, evaluation materials as well as resources produced by organisations such as Tournament of Minds, Model United Nations, Science Talent Search, Future Problem Solving and the various state gifted organisations. Resources enhance and inform the services offered to every child within a school. Opportunities to attend a host of professional learning events are an important part of providing resources for staff to learn and develop their skills. It should also be noted that the use and development of in-house experts and experiences is important in the professional learning of all staff as, like students, many staff can, and do, hide their knowledge and skills 'under a bushel'.

c. **School organistion**

    Like ICM, Renzulli recognises that there are multiple ways to organise learning. The regular curriculum can be easily influenced by SEM components by essentially challenging the academic rigour required of the learning and teaching materials. Staff development should be a major consideration in whatever mode is chosen as changes to both content and instructional methods are desired effects.

    The presence of enrichment clusters are an integral ingredient. The clusters are made up of multi-age students who share an interest. They come together during designated time blocks and work with an adult who shares their interest. It is fundamental that the adult also has expertise in the area with deep content knowledge. Essentially all work leads to the creation of a product or service. Advanced content in their field of choice, the methodology of the field and experts in the field all provides a guide to stimulate interest and talent development.

    Besides enrichment clusters, Renzulli points out that a continuum of services should be available including acceleration, mentoring with older students as well as experts from within the school community.

ICM and SEM provides just two possibilities for programming. Programs need to be influenced by the way in which a school sees their highest achieving students. The identification strategies of such students will influence who participates. The students who participate in the service need to represent the full spectrum of the school population (Renzulli, 2001); they need to be more than just the top designated percentage/s and need to be 'chosen' using more than just one type of methodology. To allow for a broad continuum of services is vital.

Whatever programming option is chosen, there is comfort in knowing that not one singular approach, definition or identification technique is better than the others. To do something has validity as doing nothing can cost a whole lot more.

CHAPTER REFERENCES

Assouline, S. G., Colangelo, N., VanTassel-Baska, J., & Lupkowski-Shoplik, A. (2015). A nation empowered: Evidence trumps the excuses holding back America's brightest students. Iowa City, IA: *Connie Belin and Jacqueline N. Blank International Center for Gifted Education and Talent Development*

Callahan, C. M. (1986). Asking the right questions: The central issue in evaluating programs for the gifted and talented. *Gifted Child Quarterly*, 30(1), 38-42

Callahan, C. M., & Reis, S. M. (Eds.). (2004). *Program evaluation in gifted education.* Corwin Press

Calvert, E. (2018). Identification and Assessment in a K-12 Talent Development Framework. 2018). *Talent Development as a Framework for Gifted Education: Implications for Best Practices and Applications in Schools.* Sourcebooks, Inc.

Colangelo, N., Assouline, S. G., & Gross, M. U. (2004). A Nation Deceived: How Schools Hold Back America's Brightest Students. The Templeton National Report on Acceleration. Volume 2. *Connie Belin & Jacqueline N. Blank International Center for Gifted Education and Talent Development* (NJ1)

Colangelo, N., et al. (2010). Guidelines for developing an academic acceleration policy. National Work Group on acceleration. *Journal of advanced academics*, 21(2), 180-203

Crockett, L. and Churches, A., 2017. *Mindful Assessment.* 1st Ed. Solution Tree.

Dettmer, Peggy (1985) Gifted program scope, structure and evaluation, *Roeper Review*, 7:3, 146-152, DOI: 10.1080/02783198509552878

Gagné, F. (2009). Building gifts into talents: Detailed overview of the DMGT 2.0. *Leading change in gifted education: The festschrift of Dr. Joyce VanTassel-Baska*, 61-80

Gagné, F. (2017). The integrative model of talent development (IMTD): In Plucker JA, Rinn AN and Makel MC From theory to educational applications. *From giftedness to gifted education: Reflecting theory in practice*, 149-182. Hawker Brownlow Education

Gilberg, J. A. (1983) Formative evaluation of gifted and talented programs, *Roeper Review*, 6:1, 43–44, DOI: 10.1080/02783198309552746

Krisel, S. C. (2018). *Programming for Talent Development Inside of School. Talent Development as a Framework for Gifted Education: Implications for Best Practices and Applications in Schools.* Sourcebooks, Inc.

Nottingham, J. (2017). *The learning challenge: How to guide your students through the learning pit to achieve deeper understanding.* Corwin Press

Olszewski-Kubilius, P., Subotnik, R., & Worrell, F. (2018). *Talent development as a framework for gifted education: Implications for best practices and applications in schools.* Sourcebooks, Inc.

Renzulli, J. and Reis, S., (2014). *The Schoolwide Enrichment Model. A How-to Guide for Talent Development.*1st ed. Waco Texas: Prufock Press

Renzulli, J. S. (2012). Reexamining the role of gifted education and talent development for the 21st century: A four-part theoretical approach. *Gifted Child Quarterly*, 56(3), 150–159

Renzulli, J. S. (2001). Gifted education in the new century: Identification and Programming issues. *Australasian Journal of Gifted Education.* 10. 23–32. Updated 2017 by author

Rogers, K. B. (1993). Grouping the gifted and talented: Questions and answers. *Roeper Review*, 16(1), 8–12

Rogers, K. B. (2002). R*e-forming gifted education: Matching the program to the child.* Great Potential Press, Inc.

Rogers, K. B. (2017) Brushing up your program of service. WCGTC Conference Paper Sydney 2017

Schroth, S. T. (2013). Service delivery models. *Critical issues and practices in gifted education: What the research says*, 577–591

Silverman, L. (2013). *Giftedness 101.* New York, NY: Springer Pub. Co

Tomlinson, C. A. (2009). Myth 8: The "Patch-On" Approach to Programming Is Effective. *Gifted Child Quarterly*, 53(4), 254–256. https://doi.org/10.1177/0016986209346931

VanTassel-Baska, J., & Little, C. A. (2017). Content-Based Curriculum for High-Ability Learners. Sourcebooks, Inc.. VanTassel-Baska, J., & Little, C. A. (2016). *Content-Based Curriculum for High-Ability Learners.* Hawker Brownlow Education

Worrell, F. C., Subotnik, R. F., Olszewski-Kubilius, P., & Dixson, D. D. (2019). Gifted students. *Annual review of psychology*, 70, 551–576

CHAPTER 7

CURRICULUM DIFFERENTIATION FOR GIFTED STUDENTS IN SECONDARY SCIENCE CLASSES

CHRISTINE IRELAND

This chapter provides guidance for teachers about addressing the academic needs of highly-able students in mixed-ability classes. It argues that identifying these students and understanding their needs requires adequate teacher professional development. It questions whether adequate student input is being accessed with regard to this issue

WHY IS EFFECTIVE CURRICULUM DIFFERENTIATION SO IMPORTANT FOR GIFTED SECONDARY SCIENCE STUDENTS?

Highly-able students under-achieving is a serious issue (Colangelo, Assouline, & Gross, 2004; Emerick, 1992; Reis & McCoach, 2000; Whitmore, 1980). Gifted underachievers are recognised, and turned around, by appropriate curriculum differentiation (Tomlinson et al., 2003). Gifted underachievement has an impact on all students, and on the wider community. Appropriate curriculum differentiation improves individual students' engagement and performance levels. It contributes to better classroom behaviour, and higher levels of individual advancement. Teachers are enabled by using successful gifted education curriculum differentiation strategies, schools are improved through whole-school programming for gifted students, and at-risk gifted underachievers are empowered through recognition and authentic progress. However, gifted students' scores have been decreasing for decades in Australia (Buckingham, 2016; Masters, 2013, 2015, 2016). According to Munro (2020), the skill level of gifted students currently "is usually devalued or even ignored in schools".

Curriculum differentiation is not easy to achieve, especially in a secondary, mixed ability classroom. Masters (2015) indicated that the wide spread of ability levels in these classrooms makes achieving effective curriculum differentiation, especially for high-ability students, extremely difficult. Despite the focus that schools place on curriculum differentiation, its achievability is therefore highly questionable (Archambault et al., 1993; Benny & Blonder, 2016; Berger, 1991; Feldhusen & Kroll, 1991; Reis & McCoach, 2000; Watters & Diezmann, 2003).

WHY IS IT IMPORTANT TO LOOK AT WHAT IS HAPPENING TO GIFTED STUDENTS IN SCIENCE CLASSES?

ACARA (2015) determined that highly-able students need harder work academically, that pushes them beyond what they can already do. That places them above their chronological age peers, and as mentioned, creates the incoorect thinking from some teachers that the provision of different academic work is somehow unfair. VanTassel-Baska and MacFarlane (2008) contended that acceleration for these students is needed: "Early access to advanced science content appears to be a desirable option for gifted learners".

Not enough has been done to research this issue: "Although the literature is replete with models and advice on the education of gifted students, there are few examples of good practice applied to science" (Watters &

Diezmann, 2003). Interestingly, science is a subject perfect for practical extension of highly-able students, as it offers hands on activities and creative problem-solving. Often this subject is dealing with critical worldwide problems (Poncini & Poncini, 2002) that would be of real importance to enquiring minds. Omdal and Richards (2008) noted that science fairs and competitions particularly benefited highly-able students. These events "raised their awareness of educational possibilities, increased their confidence, validated their exceptional ability, and helped them set higher goals for their futures". It is unfortunate that the Australian Programme for International Student Assessment (PISA), the Trends in International Mathematics and Science Study (TIMSS) and NAPLAN results show that Australian students' achievement levels have been decreasing, especially for the more highly-able students, for three decades. At the same time, Australian science teachers' understanding of best curriculum differentiation practice for secondary science students is inadequate (Ireland et al., 2020).

Engagement levels for highly-able students in science classes is a problem (Gubbins et al., 2013). Yazzie-Mintz (2010) examined highly-able students' perceptions of how challenged they were in class. The results were appalling. Less than 50 percent felt challenged in their classes, 25 percent felt challenged academically in 'none' or only '1 or 2' classes, and 63 percent stated that hard work was expected in either 'none', or in only '1 or 2' of their classes. How curriculum differentiation is being used to extend gifted students in Science classes is therefore a critically important issue.

Science education reform for gifted students is overdue. Schools commonly work from a mixed-ability classroom context. Acceleration and ability grouping options are not common practice. Ability grouping provides strong gains for gifted students (Gross, 1997). Lynch (1994) noted that "grouping practices alone are unlikely to influence science education reform unless considered in the context of comprehensive restructuring efforts at the local school level". Whole school reform and effective leadership are required. VanTassel-Baska and MacFarlane (2008) contended that "gifted learners at secondary levels appear to benefit from advanced instruction in science, consistent with their levels of functioning in the subject, but beyond the typical level of science offered by the school". Educators must become more aware of how under-challenged their highly-able students are feeling (Watters & Diezmann, 2003). Evidence has been collected (Ireland et al, 2020) showing that Australian highly-able secondary Science students perceive that curriculum differentiation strategies are not being successfully provided: "In particular, some strategies requiring modification of the learning environment were considered by highly-able students to be significantly less frequently achieved, compared to teachers' perceptions". The attitude from a minority of ill-informed educators, that gifted education options are a form of elitism, must not be supported in any way (Nikakis, 2012).

WHAT DOES CURRICULUM DIFFERENTIATION FOR HIGHLY-ABLE STUDENTS LOOK LIKE IN A SCIENCE CLASSROOM?

As for any classroom, extension requires that academic rigour be essential, not optional. According to Kingore (2013), educators need to increase rigour to reverse students' thinking, from aiming at 'the least I can do' to aiming at higher-level thinking. It is critical, however, to avoid a common mistake. Increasing rigour can unintentionally promote failure and frustration, when rigour is perceived as just more work, more difficult work, and instruction that is too fast-paced. Well planned implementation from well-trained educators is seen as key.

What is authentic rigour?
- 21st-century rigour can be defined as the ability to develop effective questions, rather than come up with only one answer. "The heart of critical thinking and problem solving is the ability to ask the right questions" (Wagner, 2008).
- Rigour involves the ability to envision oneself as a lifelong learner who is always probing, searching and exploring, and then acting on this vision.
- Rigour requires depth and complexity in learning, continual progress and striving for one's personal best.

What rigour is not, is more homework given as 'busy' work. It is not covering content more quickly, but with no greater depth. It is not requiring highly-able students to do more classwork at the basic class level, compared to the other students.

Many educators use the following three questions as tests for determining if work provided has authentic rigour for highly-able students:
1. Should every student do it?
2. Would every student want to do it?
3. Could every student do it?

The correct answer to all three questions is clearly 'no'. Increasing rigour for high-ability students requires different work, higher-level work, not just more work. Of course, curriculum compaction of the basics already acquired by the high-ability learners, would provide the time for these students to become involved in extension and enrichment. ACARA (2020) indicated that this is the right of every student: "All students are entitled to rigorous, relevant and engaging learning programs drawn from a challenging curriculum that addresses their individual learning needs". Hopefully the 2022 updated version of the Australian Curriculum will assist teachers to compact the curriculum for high-ability learners.

WHAT DOES CURRICULUM COMPACTION FOR EXTENSION LOOK LIKE IN A SCIENCE CLASSROOM?

Curriculum compacting is clearly the essential first step in developing the time and space (in a 'crowded curriculum') to achieve extension and enrichment.

An easy trick is to use an end of unit test, such as at the end of a textbook chapter, as a first activity within each unit. Then it will become clearer who knows what, and what can be compacted for each individual student. Students, especially highly-able ones, support this practice when they know the teacher is aiming to avoid repetition of already mastered knowledge. Using this same test again as part of the end of unit assessments, is then a way for all students to 'ace' their first score.

In order to provide curriculum differentiation, some teachers begin a unit with a five-minute student/teacher conference talk, in order to achieve a K–N–W Chart: What do I **K**now, **N**eed to Know & **W**ant to Know. Students begin with listing everything they know about a topic, and the five hardest things about the topic.

As practical laboratory skills always require some degree of repetition, typical practical activities for any unit could progress as planned, with perhaps some deeper enrichment and extension questioning provided for the high-ability students.

WHAT DO *EXTENSION* AND *ENRICHMENT* LOOK LIKE IN A SCIENCE CLASSROOM?

Often, working with like-minds is an important step to allow highly-able science students to experience extension and enrichment. Options that allow working with like-minds to happen, include ability or interest grouping within the classroom; interest-based withdrawal groups; electives provided by the school; bringing in older student/s; allowing a student to work with an older class at times; bringing in an expert; mentor programs; clubs; competitions; and extra-curricular activities. These types of programs have all been used to provide both extension and enrichment.

What are the blockers to this? Timetable restrictions are often cited as the reason these options cannot happen. The fact that some schools and teachers achieve these things indicates differently. There is no justice in teachers being allowed to restrict a highly-able student's progress, because they are too much of a 'tall poppy' (Nikakis, 2012), or because the role of these students is seen to be as a helper for the academically weaker students.

The difference between extension and enrichment should not dominate the issue, as both are important. Enrichment is a term that describes learning that goes beyond the general curriculum. Extension generally refers to extending learning to other content areas. Both involve learning that goes beyond the required curriculum. The difference between enrichment and extension is subtle and the two terms are often used interchangeably. For example, in a year 7 science unit on organism classification, the first step in curriculum differentiation would include identifying and framing up a significant real-world problem. This problem must be linked to a main concept in the unit, perhaps such as that thousands of plants and animals have become extinct, or are heading towards extinction, because of human intervention. Challenge the students with the 'big' questions that underlie the unit. For example, how can humans and other organisms co-exist successfully, considering humans' current rate of expansion on the planet?

These questions need to be open-ended, with no single correct answer. They are meant to stimulate inquiry, debate, and further questions. For example, consider perhaps an enrichment question in this classification unit as described above, such as "What conditions in Australia favoured marsupials?" and an extension question such as "How did plate tectonics impact marsupial development?" Enrichment and extension activities are provided to students who demonstrate mastery of basic curriculum skills and knowledge at the beginning of a unit of study, or who quickly learn new material. The purpose of enrichment and extension activities is to develop the progress of learning, and to allow students to explore their interests. More 'busy' work is not an example of enrichment or extension. Essential questions are open-ended with no single correct answer. Link the 'big question' to curriculum outcomes and indicators, and to the main facts, concepts, and skills within the unit.

CAN ACCELERATION BE IMPORTANT TO PROVIDING EXTENSION FOR HIGHLY-ABLE STUDENTS?

Gross (1999) contended that her research supported strong positive outcomes for accelerating highly-able students. However, 43 science teachers surveyed by Ireland et al. (2020) indicated teachers' clear disapproval of accelerating students, despite the fact that 161 year 7 science students surveyed were quite positive about the concept of extension for highly-able students. This challenged the work of Jaggar (1999) who researched "student perceptions of subject acceleration in NSW secondary schools" and found that "the students felt that the teachers' reception of their acceleration was 'grudging' in only 2% of cases — an encouraging indication of growing recognition of the merit of this form of acceleration". Jaggar also added that acceleration did not negatively impact highly-able students' social-emotional development. Acceleration remains an under-utilised practice in Australian education, to the detriment of our most highly-able students.

HOW DOES CREATIVE PROBLEM SOLVING (CPS) EXTEND HIGHLY-ABLE STUDENTS IN SCIENCE?

Science is an excellent subject where creative problem solving (CPS) can provide extension opportunities. As highly-able students may be working within a compacted curriculum, independent learning time would be more available for them to pursue extension activities. Whole-world problems underlying the main issues within a topic, would provide situations requiring these students to use a diverse spectrum of skills. Munro (2020) described this range of skills as including "academic, componential, verbal, visual-spatial, nonverbal, creative, performance, practical and artistic" skills.

CPS in a science learning context requires solution skills that include both practical and cognitive abilities. Munro (2020) explained these high level abilities as "action sequences in strategically advanced or superior ways to solve problems… applying and implementing what they know in novel ways". Zhang, Estabrooks, and Perry (2019) produced case-study research on bringing invention education into middle school science classrooms, using CPS techniques such as Tony Ryan's (2014) SCAMPER tool. This well-known and excellent tool provides students with innovative and challenging pathway options to solve difficult and complex problems. SCAMPER is of course an acronym to substitute or swap, combine, add, modify/magnify, put to another use, eliminate, or reverse. Current-day whole-world science problems can be tackled in this way. For example, in ACARA's (2015) year 8 science curriculum section on how animals use organs to co-ordinate their existence, solving a problem perhaps such as "How is the noise of human water-traffic negatively impacting aquatic animals?" by using the SCAMPER tool, would increase student engagement and subsequent higher-level learning. The national science curriculum provides a kaleidoscope of potential practical problem solving. Ryan's (2017) book *The Next Generation. Preparing Today's Kids for an Extraordinary Future* refers to how future creative problem-solvers will transform the planet.

Within any domain or subject area, the process of developing problem-solving action sequences within a curriculum can be achieved. Munro (2020) explained this as: "talent comes from the quality, complexity and sophistication of the action sequences they use: they solve problems by first defining and clarifying what the problem actually is; they gather relevant information and often generate multiple possible solution pathways; and they invest in the problem-solving process".

Munro (2020) suggested that this problem-solving process is a way that teachers can assess how their attempts to differentiate the curriculum have impacted highly-able students' ability to "identify and frame up the problem; describe a possible solution; compile the steps they would take to solve the problem; describe the additional information they may need to solve the problem; identify difficulties and obstacles that might make the problem hard to solve; infer how they might overcome these difficulties; identify who might be affected by the problem solving activity; describe how they could see if their solution was working". Munro (2020) has developed Makers' (1982) curriculum differentiation goals of providing analysis, synthesis, and evaluation. Determining the fundamental understandings in any unit, encourages highly-able students to enjoy solving the problems. Covid-19 is just one example of how our society very much needs the capacities of gifted and talented future problem solvers.

THE FUTURE FOR TEACHING SECONDARY SCIENCE USING CURRICULUM DIFFERENTIATION

As mentioned, mixed-ability classrooms are the most common context for all students, including high ability students. Teachers must better understand how these students think, and what skills they need. It seems that teachers too often remain unaware that their high ability students are stressed, because they are under-challenged and under-stimulated. That this problem is happening across all domains, including secondary science, is a tragic reality.

ONLINE RESOURCES USEFUL FOR PROVIDING EXTENSION

One of the most important things any teacher can do is to unreservedly share resources with colleagues. They will then decide what is useful and share these with others. Finding out what advanced programs are available for highly-able students (including tertiary options relevant to your location) is worth seeking out. The following are some online resources:

- ACARA provides on-line students' science work samples including differentiated for 'above satisfactory' levels: https://www.australiancurriculum.edu.au/resources/work-samples/portfolios/science- satisfactory-year-8/
- Ning (The Language Labyrinth)
- Google Docs, Dropbox
- Voicethread
- Glogster
- Spaaze
- TED/You Tube and other streaming media
- Jing/Screencast
- Mindmeister
- Poll Everywhere
- Issuu, ExploraTree
- Soundcloud
- Today's Meet
- Scoopit
- Khan Academy
- iTunes U
- NPR for iPad
- Developer Description
- Flipboard
- PBS Kids
- Motion Math Zoom

- Orbit Architecture
- Numbler
- Agnitus
- TeacherKit
- Solve the Outbreak

CONCLUSION

A wide range of gifted education questions have been considered in this chapter. It is clear that an appropriately differentiated education is needed for students of high ability. It is also clear that current levels of teacher professional development need improvement. It is also clear that student voice on this topic is not being adequately incorporated.

CHAPTER REFERENCES

ACARA (2015). Meeting the needs of gifted and talented students. Retrieved from https://www.australiancurriculum.edu.au/resources/student-diversity/meeting-the-needs-of-gifted-and-talented-students/

ACARA (2020). Review of the Australian Curriculum. Retrieved from https://www.acara.edu.au/curriculum/curriculum-review#:~:text=Review%20of%20the%20Australian%20Curriculum%20On%2012%20June,define%20the%20approach%20and%20scope%20of%20the%20review in the Student Diversity section (https://www.acara.edu.au/curriculum/student-diversity)

Archambault Jr, F. X., Westberg, K. L., Brown, S. W., Hallmark, B. W., Zhang, W., & Emmons, C. L. (1993). Classroom practices used with gifted third and fourth grade students. *Journal for the Education of the Gifted*, 16(2), 103–119.

Benny, N., & Blonder, R. (2016). Factors that promote/inhibit teaching gifted students in a regular class: Results from a professional development program for chemistry teachers. *Education Research International*. Article ID 2742905. doi: 10.1155/2016/2742 905

Berger S. L. (1991). *Differentiating curriculum for gifted students* (Digest #E510). Reston, VA: The Council for Exceptional Children. (ERIC Document Reproduction Service No. ED34217591)

Colangelo, N., Assouline, S. G., & Gross, M.U.M. (2004). *A Nation Deceived: How schools hold back America's Brightest Students*. Iowa City: University of Iowa.

Emerick, L.J. (1992). Academic underachievement among the gifted: Students' perceptions of factors that reverse the pattern. *Gifted Child Quarterly*. 36, 140–146

Feldhusen, J.F., & Kroll, M.D. (1991). Boredom or challenge for the academically talented in school. *Gifted Education International*, 7, 80-81

Gross, M.U.M. (1997). To group or not to group: Is that the question. *Gifted* (April), 25-29

Gross, M.U.M. (1999). From the "saddest sound" to the D Major chord: The gift of accelerated progression. Presented at the 3rd Biennial Australian International Conference on the Education of Gifted Students, Melbourne, Australia. [Online]. Retrieved from: https://www.hoagiesgifted.org/d_major_chord.htm

Gubbins, E., Villanueva, M., Gilson, C., Foreman, J., Bruce-Davis, M., & Vahidi,S. (2013). Status of STEM High Schools and implications for practice (Unpublished manuscript). University of Connecticut, Storrs, CT

Ireland, C., Bowles, T. V., Brindle, K. A., & Nikakis, S. (2020). Curriculum differentiation's capacity to extend gifted students in secondary mixed-ability science classes, *Talent*, 10(1), 21-42

Jaggar, K. A. (1999). Student perceptions of subject acceleration in New South Wales secondary schools. University of New South Wales

Kingore, B. W. (2013). *Rigor and engagement for growing minds: Strategies that enable high-ability learners to flourish in all classrooms.* PA Publishing

Lynch, S. (1994). Ability grouping and science education reform: Policy and research base. *Journal of Research in Science Teaching*, 31(2), 105-128

Masters, G. (2013). *Reforming educational assessment: Imperatives, principles and challenges.* Camberwell, Vic: ACER Press

Masters, G. (2015). Challenging our most able students. *Teacher Magazine*. Retrieved from https://www.teachermagazine.com.au/geoff-masters/.../challenging-our-most able-students

Masters, G. (2016). Retrieved from final paragraph in https://teachforaustralia.org/2016/12/07/australias-pisa-results-show-educational-disadvantage-gap-remains/

Munro, J. (2020). Resource Keynote. What Does Gifted Practical Learning Look Like in the Classroom? *Vision*, 31(2), 10-13

Nikakis, S. (2012). Why do we need to advocate for gifted students? In *Let the Tall Poppies Flourish: Advocating to Achieve Educational Justice for all Gifted Students.* (pp. 1-10). Heidelberg Press

Omdal, S. N., & Richards, M. R. E., (2008). Academic Competitions. In J. Plucker & C. Callahan. (Eds.). *Critical issues and practices* (pp. 5-13). Waco, Texas: Prufrock Press Inc.

Poncini, A., & Poncini, L., (2002). A qualitative assessment of gifted and talented students undertaking research science projects. In W. Vialle & J. Geake (Eds), *The gifted enigma. A collection of articles.* Victoria, Australia. Hawker Brownlow (pp. 20-41)

Reis, S.M., & McCoach, D.B. (2000). The underachievement of gifted students: What do we know and where do we go? *Gifted Child Quarterly*, 44, 152–170

Ryan, T. (2014) *Thinkers Keys: A Powerful Program for Teaching Children to Become Extraordinary Thinkers*. HeadFirst Publications, Mt Gravatt, Queensland

Ryan, T. (2017) *The Next Generation. Preparing Today's Kids for an Extraordinary Future*. Wiley and Sons Publishers, Toronto, Canada

Tomlinson, C. A., Brighton, C., Hertberg, H., Callahan, C. M., Moon, T. R., Brimijoin, K., Conover, L. & Reynolds, T. (2003). Differentiating instruction in response to student readiness, interest, and learning profile in academically diverse classrooms: A review of literature. *Journal for the Education of the Gifted*, 27(2–3), 119–145. Retrieved from: https://files.eric.ed.gov/fulltext/EJ787917.pdf

VanTassel-Baska, J. & MacFarlane, B. (2008). Science, Secondary. In J. A. Plucker & C. M. Callahan (Eds.), *Critical issues and practices in gifted education: What the research says* (p. 579–593). Waco, TX: Prufrock Press

Wagner, T. (2008). Rigor redefined. *Educational leadership*, 66(2), 20–24.

Watters, J.J., & Diezmann, C.M (2003). The gifted student in science: Fulfilling potential. *Australian Science Teachers Journal*, 49(3), 46–53. Retrieved from: https://eprints.qut.edu.au/1692/1/1692.pdf

Whitmore, J. (1980) *Giftedness, conflict and underachievement*. Boston, MA: Allyn and Baker

Yazzie-Mintz, E. (2010). Charting the path from engagement to achievement: A report on the 2009 high school survey of student engagement. Bloomington, IN: Indiana University. Center for Evaluation and Education Policy.

Zhang, H., Estabrooks, L., & Perry, A. (2019). Bringing invention education into middle school science classrooms: a case study. *Technology & Innovation*, 20(3), 235–250

CHAPTER 8

DIFFERENTIATING LEARNING WITH STEM EDUCATION INQUIRY PROJECTS PART ONE – THEORY

SHELLEY WALDON

Well-designed science, technology, engineering, and mathematics (STEM) Education Inquiry Projects provide learning opportunities for students at all levels of capacity and engagement. When a project is initiated with a strong accessible provocation or contentious issue, which allows students to engage with topics of interest to them, then self-differentiation will occur. An open design brief with multiple potential solutions encourages students to enter at their own level and enables extensive exploration for all students. Gifted and high-achieving students can benefit significantly from open-ended inquiries that extend them beyond specific curriculum domains in which they're academically advanced and highly successful, by broadening their capabilities and skills and expanding their thinking.

> **Vignette 1 – Lucas (Year 9 – a Catholic co-ed regional college)**
>
> *"Lucas was a student who had been underachieving in maths classes for the last couple of years upon enrolment into our STEM: Experiments in space class. Lucas had completed a variety of maths units on trigonometry and algebra, but had failed to grasp both the concept and purpose of both topics, which was confirmed by his parents in a parent teacher interview. As part of our rocketry unit within the subject students covered these topics again, but with the context of calculating apogees, speed and acceleration of rockets. Towards the end of the unit more advanced algebraic equations such as Barrowman's were introduced to students, and with the purpose of the mathematics seen, Lucas was a willing engager with these equations."* Head of science & STEM leader
>
> When I interviewed Lucas I found him articulate and confident when discussing his ideas about designing combination rocket propulsion systems. I asked him about his maths challenges and his comments were that he struggled with maths based on what his maths teacher had said, however when he showed me the complex maths he was undertaking in the rockets elective and I pointed out that it was 2-3 years in advance of his current level, his comment was that, "Oh! But those equations are easy because its rocket maths".
>
> **Reflection:** Within a real context of personal interest, Lucas not only had no problems with the maths but demonstrated a superior understanding of the concepts and capacity to solve complex specialist algebraic equations. He's not empirically 'bad' at maths – he struggles with school maths.

> *"Every maker of video games knows something that the makers of curriculum don't seem to understand. You'll never see a video game being advertised as being easy. Kids who do not like school will tell you it's not because it's too hard. It's because it's ... boring"*
> (Papert, 1993)

Creating leaning experiences for all students, which provide opportunities in which they're motivated to engage with the curriculum content, make meaning of concepts and build understanding, requires mindfulness of contemporary understanding of how children learn. For gifted students in particular, it is essential that teachers develop the capacity to perceive the nuances and apply appropriate practice which can extend students in their areas of talent. Often students are accelerated into higher grades for one of more areas in which they demonstrate understanding beyond their peers at the same level. Whilst this may provide the interest and motivation for some students to continue to extend their learning, there are also challenges to be overcome in the social domains.

For students that are gifted in the readily measurable academic disciplines, such as literacy and numeracy, they may not have the opportunity to develop matching social and complementary skills that maintain motivation or engagement with the content. Much research confirms that many talented students fail to flourish at school and don't achieve their potential. Some gifted students may hide their talents and 'dumb down' to fit in with their peers, or become bored with revisiting content that they've already fully integrated into their understanding, whilst at the same time failing to develop other life skills.

> *"If these students who have clearly demonstrated their ability to go beyond the regular curriculum…are not given a different type of curriculum, they may languish in boredom in school and fail to develop their potential"* (Dixon, 2006)

At the 2016 Australian Council of Educational Research Conference (Improving STEM Learning: What will it take?), Geoff Masters presented his policy insights into the current challenges in Australian education (O'Connell, 2019). He specifically targeted the diminishing standards and engagement of Australian students in the STEM discipline areas and the impact that will have in the future. He reflected on policies driving current curriculum development and delivery models in Australian schools and highlighted the ongoing impacts and disadvantages for many secondary students of existing learning models and environments, in particular:

- Current curricula are often dominated by substantial bodies of factual and procedural knowledge, at a time when it is increasingly important that students can apply deep understandings of key disciplinary concepts and principles to real-world problems

- School subjects tend to be taught in isolation from each other, at a time when solutions to societal challenges and the nature of work are becoming increasingly cross-disciplinary
- School curricula often emphasise passive, reproductive learning and the solution of standard problem types, at a time when there is a growing need to promote creativity and the ability to develop innovative solutions to entirely new problems
- Assessment processes – especially in senior secondary school – tend to provide information about subject achievement only; at a time when employers are seeking better information about students' abilities to work in teams, use technology, communicate, solve problems and learn on the job
- Students – especially in senior secondary school – often learn in isolation and in competition with each other; at a time when workplaces are increasingly being organised around teamwork and are requiring good interpersonal and communication skills
- School curricula tend to be designed for delivery in traditional classroom settings, at a time when new technologies are transforming how courses are delivered and learning takes place (Masters, 2016).

He advocated for a shift in focus to a curriculum that prepares students for life and work, promoting cross-disciplinary, team-based problem-solving learning opportunities that provide:
- Deep understanding of subject matter and the ability to apply what is learnt
- Ability to communicate and solve problems in teams
- Ability to think critically and to create innovative, novel solutions
- Flexibility, openness to change and a willingness to learn continually.

The expanding value of the general capabilities as part of life-long learning has been recognised across the range of educational stakeholders, impacting policy decisions and to varying extents being embedded in the curriculum. The 'Beyond ATAR' report (2019) proposed changes to assessment, beyond reliance on high stakes testing as entry points to tertiary education or employment. The objective is to provide senior students with a learner profile, including strengths in the capabilities as well as academic performance in the disciplines. This model of credentialing is already in existence in some school networks, including the International Baccalaureate, the New Tech Network, and Big Picture Education Australia. These types of educational institutes and networks, rely on the teacher acting as facilitator of learning and providing or negotiating student mentors and opportunities for internships in organisations that meet their individual students' needs. They promote student exploration of topics of interest to them and require a demonstration or performance of understanding as part of assessment.

Discipline based learning vs cross-disciplinary learning is not a zero-sum game. A recent report from Milligan (2020), focused on the importance of the skills and attributes within the capabilities, as well as mastery in discipline areas. She stated that the institutions, school networks and potential employers, *"... did not see subject mastery as an alternative or in competition. Developing expertise and real depth in mastery of a domain, subject or discipline goes hand-in-hand with developing general, transferable learning capabilities. You simply do not get excellence in one without excellence in the other."*

IDEO Chairman Tim Brown popularised the concept of a T-shaped person as an ideal employee, because they combine two types of characteristics:
1. Deep discipline understanding and expertise in a specific field (the upright or I), with
2. Cross-disciplinary competencies, (the cross-bar of the T) which involve a broad set of skills including understanding of contexts, disposition to collaborate and capacity to communicate.

This combination is significant, since deep knowledge is of little value, without the aptitude to apply it in specific contexts and be able to share and communicate to an audience. Conversely, a willingness to collaborate and communicate without something of value to communicate and bring to creating a solution to a challenge, is also of little extrinsic value.

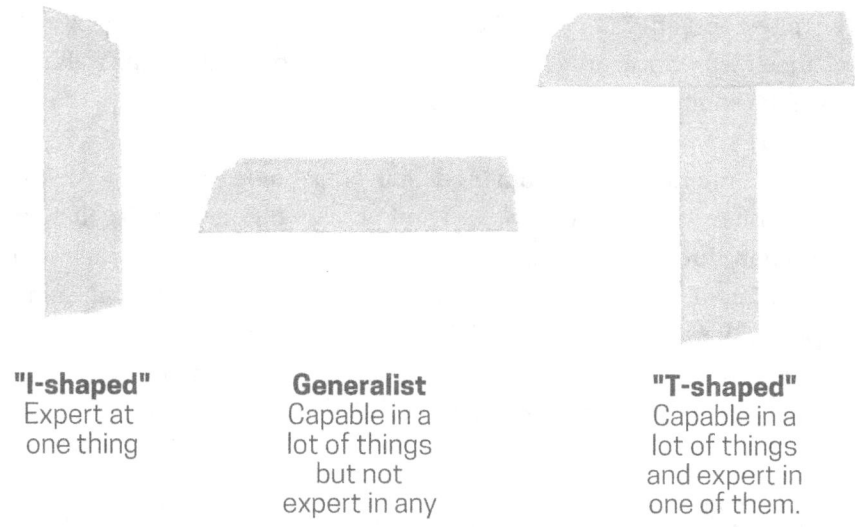

"I-shaped"	**Generalist**	**"T-shaped"**
Expert at one thing	Capable in a lot of things but not expert in any	Capable in a lot of things and expert in one of them.

Figure 1: I-shaped vs Generalist vs T-shaped (Yip, 2018)

Ideally the aspiration of teachers for extending and supporting the full growth of their gifted students, should be developing a breadth of skills and familiarity with general knowledge outside their core discipline, to complement their talent in particular domains. Milligan (2020), reflects that a number of change actions need to take place in schools and their learning and teaching philosophies to effect these aspirations and develop the successful citizens for the future:

- Students have to be given opportunities to learn and demonstrate their capabilities. They need opportunities to think for themselves, develop critical faculties and test claims and evidence outside their own sphere of experience.
- Learners need free rein to communicate, and collaborate with others to build knowledge, solve problems or generate creative solutions to complex issues that might not have been tackled before.
- They need the opportunity to direct their own learning, free of directive teaching. Their passions and interests, and capacity for perseverance must be allowed to flower.

- They must also have the opportunity to express social and community values and ethics in both thought and deed – taking responsibility for their own work to produce, create, build, and contribute to the wellbeing of the community (Milligan, 2020).

In contemporary classrooms, digital technologies offer multiple opportunities for teachers to design and prepare differentiated, self-paced instruction through blended or hybrid learning experiences, which allow mastery for all. Sometimes called the 'flipped classroom' is where teachers prepare videos or screencasts of the content and students can access as frequently as needed so the teacher can focus on clarifying misconceptions. The modern classrooms approach is indicated in figure 2.

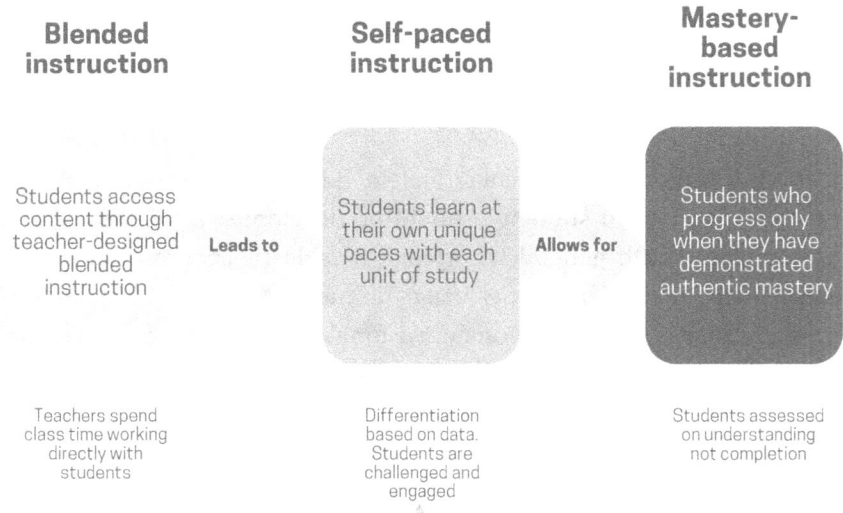

Figure 2: Contemporary instructional approach – Modern classrooms (https://modernclassrooms.org/approach)

Well-designed, integrated STEM education inquiries, can combine all these practices and offer students the opportunity to flourish and grow into T-shaped people, rather than becoming social outliers, on the continuum from introspective 'nerds' to those exhibiting anti-social behaviours to offset boredom.

STEM EDUCATION

> "STEM education is a term used to refer collectively to the teaching of the disciplines within its umbrella – science, technology, engineering and mathematics – and also to a cross-disciplinary approach to teaching that increases student interest in STEM-related fields and improves students' problem solving and critical analysis skills. STEM sits within a broader foundational knowledge base and the teaching of STEM is a part, albeit important, of a balanced program of learning." (National STEM School Education Strategy, 2016–2026).

STEM education can empower pedagogical practices for creating opportunities to contextualise learning, integrating disciplinary skills and knowledge applied in real world contexts. Capabilities of ethical thinking and acting for justice and the common good can be incorporated.

In best practice, STEM education is not situated purely within the discipline domains of the curriculum but is a combination of the content knowledge within the disciplines and the skills within the capabilities curriculum. Shulman (1986) defined pedagogical content knowledge (PCK) as a very specific form of teacher knowledge of practice, selecting a particular way of teaching discipline concepts, explicitly designed to enhance students' ability to understand and learn as needed. The PCK of the teacher is an essential component, being strategically deployed to optimise the learning for all students. (Figure 3 overleaf provides a visual summary).

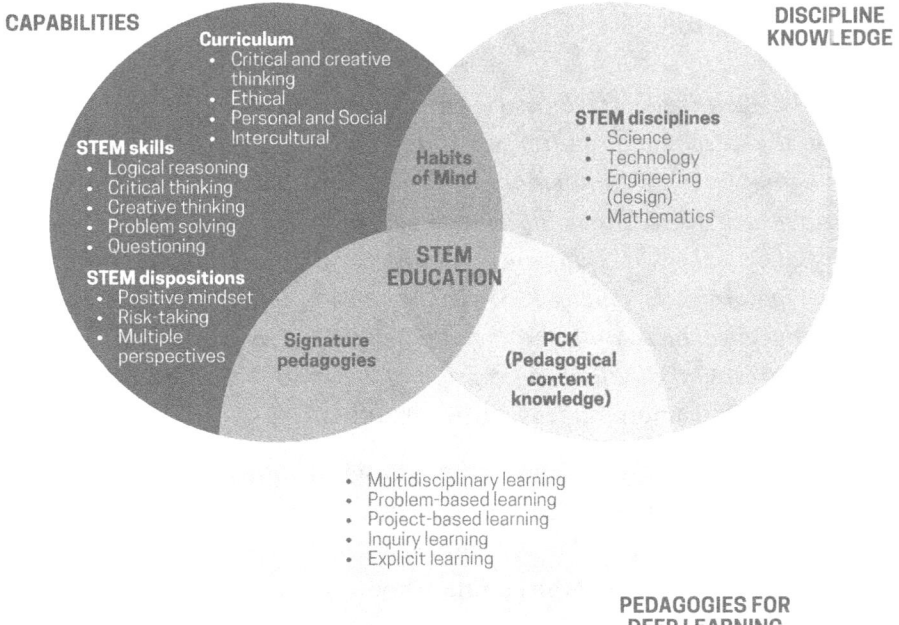

Figure 3: STEM education visual (prepared by Waldon, 2017)

A STEM education inquiry is not a study within a single discipline area. At the minimum, it combines opportunities to learn within two disciplines; functions well combining three disciplines; and optimally can be designed to combine all four of the disciplines. Science and mathematics provide the conceptual and content based dimensions and engineering (design) provides the experience in which the science is explored and the mathematics applied. Technology is ideally an enabler of learning at every stage of the process.

There are vocal advocates for incorporating other elements of the curriculum into STEM and schools select models that suit their contexts, including eSTEM, STEAM, STEAMD, SHTREAM, STEMM, g-STEM. (We recommend you Google these to see how they all differ.) Whilst a sufficiently open STEM inquiry project can accommodate the arts, humanities, religion, etc.; at its core, it should be primarily directed towards the application of science and mathematics concepts to address challenges and solve problems.

The combination of the discipline areas in defining STEM Education has also been variously referred to as interdisciplinary, cross-disciplinary, multi-disciplinary, transdisciplinary amongst the most common descriptors. Vasquez et al. (2013) framed a continuum of increasing levels of integration visualised in figure 4.

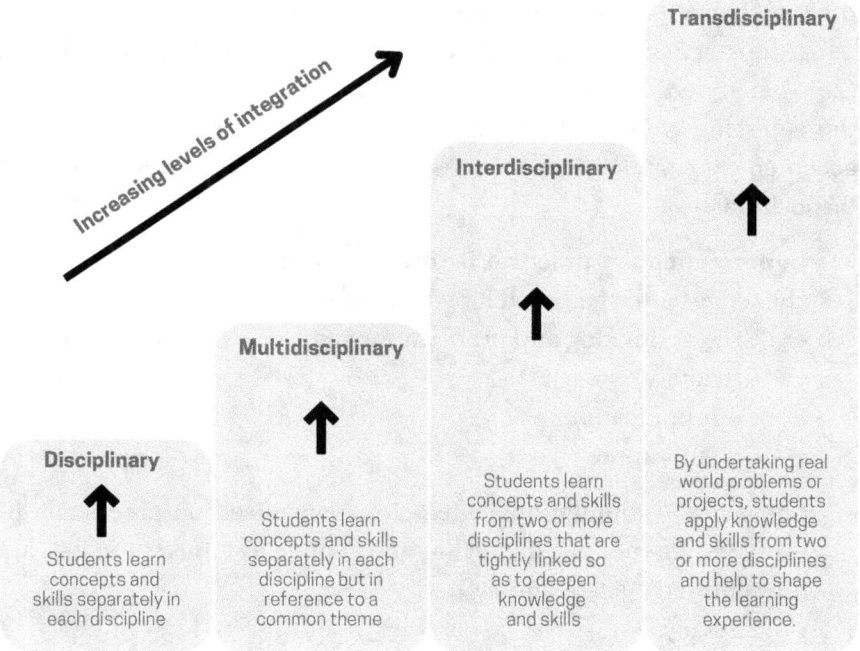

Figure 4: The inclined plane of STEM integration
(Vasquez, Sneider and Comer, 2013)

This continuum is also reflected in the level of teacher direction and release of responsibility in inquiry projects; progressing from teacher designed and directed, framing the question and setting the project; through a guided inquiry model of choice within clearly set parameters; up to fully student directed inquiries. Students need to develop the skill set to move along this continuum through carefully scaffolded learning experiences over time.

Within STEM education programs learners also need chances to develop the complementary set of 21st-century skills. These skills are variously labelled enterprise and transferable skills as they are not discipline specific and cross learning areas. They are sometimes (inappropriately) labelled 'soft' skills, which can diminish perceptions of their importance. These capabilities include critical and creative thinking, collaboration and communication amongst a variety of literacies and personal and social competencies. These skills are the broad capabilities which form the crossbar of the T-shaped person. Across the range of the numerous definitions of 21st-century skills a report to the World Economic Forum (2016) analysed the future focussed skills student will need to thrive in the emerging globalised society. They were organised into 3 generally accepted categories: competencies, literacies and character qualities or dispositions:

- **Competencies** – practical learning and thinking skills to address challenges often gathered for convenience as the 4Cs
  - Critical thinking and problem solving
  - Creativity
  - Communication
  - Collaboration

- **Literacies** – foundational literacies, recognised as core skills for everyday life (not just digital literacy as often assumed in STEM; and now embracing data literacy)
  - Literacy
  - Numeracy
  - Scientific literacy
  - ICT literacy
  - Financial literacy
  - Cultural and civic literacy

- **Dispositions** – personal attitudes about building resilience and approaching social and cultural challenges
  - Curiosity
  - Initiative
  - Persistence/grit
  - Adaptability
  - Leadership
  - Social and cultural awareness

Vignette 2 – Myra (Years 7–9 – a Catholic girl's school)

A group of extension students had been working together on our first STEM project. Students had been researching endangered species in south-eastern Australia. With puppets that they designed and constructed themselves, they performed a puppet show to entertain and educate young audiences about the plight of these endangered species.

One of the students, Myra, had been devoting hours to the project and her skills in both design and construction were developing extremely well. The day to attend the STEM MAD Showcase (for Melbourne Archdiocese Catholic Schools) was rapidly approaching and there was great excitement. The girls were very aware that they would have to be ready, on the day, to speak to members of various judging panels as well as other visitors to our booth. Myra, despite all of her hard work, did not want to attend the day as she was fearful of speaking in public. After much persuasion by myself and her teammates, Myra agreed to be there on the day, although she assured us that she would quietly stand in the background. On the day, however, Myra was asked a direct question and after some hesitation, she answered. Myra's months of preparation had provided her with a strong understanding and knowledge. Her answer surprised her and her teammates praised her. After a few more questions the judging panel arrived. Myra then took charge. She spoke with assurance, authority and in an engaging manner. Myra continued to be the main speaker of the day and the other girls deferred to her when questions were asked.

On the bus ride home the girls were jubilant. Myra, in particular, was in great spirits. She had overcome a fear and had been greatly successful.

"This experience in STEM provided Myra with the opportunity for growth. Myra had been using and developing important skills for this 21st century: collaboration, critical and creative thinking, perseverance, leadership and communication." – Head of science and STEM elective leader

> I had the opportunity to meet Myra at a variety of STEM showcases over 3 years and I always found her excited by her learning and articulate in sharing. When challenged to tease out the nuances of her learning, her depth of understanding and conceptual knowledge was well advanced and she was able to demonstrate a capacity to link ideas and transfer her knowledge which was well in advance of her years. Despite being in external and unfamiliar environments she was confident and comfortable to express herself in front of her peers and unknown educators.
>
> **Reflection:** With a keen understanding of the students in her care and recognising the barriers, Myra's teacher was able to provide the encouragement and support needed to both engage and extend her to her potential. Under this supportive regime and scaffolded series of experiences, including strategic questioning, Myra has flourished and successfully developed her confidence in her abilities. In increasingly challenging environments, Myra has demonstrated to herself and others her superior content knowledge and understanding.

GENDER BASED ISSUES

Helen Watt (2016) reported on a 20-year longitudinal study examining and comparing the motivation and engagement of boys and girls in specific subject areas, including the STEM subjects. She explored the influences and learning environments, which differentially impact girls continued participation in the senior sciences and mathematics and how they are disadvantaged by prematurely dropping out of the 'STEM pipeline' (The STEM Pipeline is a term used in policy documents and discussions to describe the educational pathways which exist for students in the STEM fields, leading to participation opportunities in STEM careers).

Within the educational life of students there are important moments of self-selection, where students make decisions that both drive forward and restrict their choices in their learning trajectory. For example, whether students enjoy reading for its own sake or make assumptions about their capability and thus liking for mathematics, often becomes apparent at about the grade 3 to 4 level, when the curriculum complexities start to really differentiate students' locations on the learning continuum. Watt (2016) found that by end of grade 6 and at entry into secondary school, students' attitudes and self-belief in their mathematical skills was fixed and this becomes a critical filter in their progression through mathematics based learning areas, particularly influencing their choices of participation in senior STEM disciplines. She identified the *"... most proximal predictors of achievement-related choices are self-belief and task values."* Task values included social perceptions of purpose and relevance of science and mathematics activities, as significant influences on motivation, particularly for girls. She noted that girls were inspired by tasks they found socially meaningful and driven by issues related to social justice.

Additionally for girls, in early secondary schooling as they reach puberty, their self-confidence also becomes a limiting factor in their self-belief about their mathematical skills. They are also readily influenced by their peers and the decision to pursue senior STEM disciplines, even when they're demonstrably capable of succeeding, is often weighed in an inaccurately framed zero-sum analysis, against the perceptions of time needed to get good marks in 'harder' subjects and the fear of becoming socially isolated. In a series of informal 'vox pops' (Vox populi – in journalism the 'man on the street' is a short interviews or questionnaire, to gain the general opinion or belief about a subject), which I conducted with female undergraduates in engineering schools and female engineers, the overwhelming attitude to their participation in engineering was that they had succeeded despite their schooling not because of their schooling. The intrinsic drivers for these girls were a love of the sciences and an insatiable curiosity about how things work, which overrode negative social perceptions about the participation of girls in what had historically been primarily male dominated careers and pursuits.

Watt's findings suggested that to redress the gender imbalance in pursuit of STEM related careers and participation in sciences and mathematics, teachers could:
- Introduce students to positive role models
- Make explicit connections between the social uses and purposes of STEM concepts and skills
- Create learning environments that positively impact students' self-concepts and values
- Design learning opportunities which engage students with real issues and problems, requiring solutions that entail acting for justice and the common good.

CHAPTER REFERENCES

Catholic Education Melbourne (2015). T*o Serve and Lead: CEM Strategic Plan 2015-2019*. Melbourne: Catholic Education Melbourne

Catholic Education Melbourne (2016, September). *Horizons of Hope: Curriculum Foundation Statement*. Retrieved from Catholic Education Victoria Network (CEVN): https://cevn.cecv.catholic.edu.au/Melb/Curriculum/Horizons-of-Hope/Strategy-Statements

Catholic Education Melbourne (2016, September). *Horizons of Hope: Pedagogy Foundation Statement*. Retrieved from Catholic Education Victoria Network: https://cevn.cecv.catholic.edu.au/Melb/Curriculum/Horizons-of-Hope/Strategy-Statements

Dixon, F. A. (2006). Critical thinking: A foundation for challenging content. In F. Dixon, *The handbook of secondary gifted education* (pp. 323-341). Waco, TX: Prufrock Press

Masters, G. N. (2016). Five challenges in Australian school education. *Policy Insights Issue 5*. Camberwell, VIC: ACER

Milligan, S. (2020, June 29). *Future proofing Australian students with 'new credentials'.* Retrieved from Pursuit - University of Melbourne: https://pursuit.unimelb.edu.au/articles/future-proofing-australian-students-with-new-credentials

O'Connell, M. M. (2019, September). *Beyond ATAR: a proposal for change*. Australian Learning Lecture. Melbourne, Victoria: Koshland Innovation Fund. Retrieved from Austrlaina Learning Lecture: https://all-learning.org.au/beyond-atar/

Papert, S. (1993). *The Children's Machine: Rethinking school in the age of the computer.* New York: Basic Books

Shulman, L. (1986). Those Who Understand: Knowledge Growth in Teaching. *Educational Researcher*, Vol.15, No.2, 4-14

Vasquez, A. S. (2013). *STEM Lesson Essentials, Grades 3-8: Integrating Science, Technology, Engineering and Mathematics.* New York: Heinemann

Watt, H. (2016). Promoting girls' and boys' engagement and particaption in senior secondary STEM fields and occupational aspirations. *ACER Research Conference - Improving STEM Learning: What will it take?* (pp. 34-44). Brisbane: Australian Council for Educational Research

World Economic Forum in collaboaration with The Boston Consulting Group. (2016). *New Vision for Education: Fostering Social and Emotional Learning through Technology.* World Economic Forum

Yip, J. (2018, March 25). *Why T-shaped people?* Retrieved from medium.com

CHAPTER 9

DIFFERENTIATING LEARNING WITH STEM EDUCATION INQUIRY PROJECTS
PART TWO – PRACTICE

SHELLEY WALDON

Curriculum design in a Catholic school positions learning as connected rather than discrete isolated elements. It connects big ideas, concepts and thinking ...
– Horizons of Hope: Curriculum Statement (CEM, 2016)

DESIGNING LEARNING FOR STEM EDUCATION

In designing engaging curriculum experiences for gifted students, STEM education can offer:
- a strong vision for integrated education that is underpinned by deep knowledge, understanding of research and system directions and a recognition of context

- teachers as designers of learning who promote collaboration and problem solving as essential learning capabilities for themselves and their students and ensure equitable access and opportunity for all.

An integrated STEM education inquiry can be designed to address the requirements of the curriculum through a variety of approaches. Figure 1 compares several of the most well-researched, established approaches which can be positioned in two different forms of methodology:

1. The curriculum is used to formulate the inquiry and an appropriate learning sequence is applied to set the curriculum in a context that makes connections to students' lives and interests.
2. An authentic problem or challenge to be solved drives the inquiry and the teacher identifies the areas of the curriculum which can be readily tackled through the project process and makes the connections to student learning.

STEM Education Methodologies - A Comparison of Approaches, Philosophies and Sequences of Learning

	Design approaches (can be bounded by a problem seeking a solution)						Inquiry approaches (can be bounded by curriculum)		
	Integrated STEM Inquiry Process[1]	Engineering Design Process[2]	Project Based Learning[3]	Design Thinking Process[4]	LAUNCH Cycle[5]	Solution Frequency	Inquiry Learning[6]	5 E's[7]	Scientific Method[8]
Learning Intention	Using integrated, multidisciplinary learning opportunities, students develop skills in problem solving, critical & creative thinking.	To engineer research-informed products to solve real-world problems through an iterative cycle of prototyping and testing	To drive authentic deep learning to develop research-informed responses to a provocation or contentious issue	To create novel, research-informed solutions to complex, real-world challenges from a human-centred perspective. The challenge may be defined by the students or pre-determined by a primary stakeholder through a design brief			To develop answers to rich questions through a process of exploration, research and evaluation		To investigate the relationship between an independent and dependent variable by collecting and analysing data to support or refute a hypothesis
Outcomes	Student agency is enabled with engagement and motivation to learn	A product/solution that best meets the problem specifications	Authentic public demonstration of deep learning and student ownership of problem	Implement innovative solutions to human-centred challenges through a set of designated stages of thinking and doing.			Integrates concepts from across the curriculum to take action that matters	Articulate refined, research-informed answers to rich questions	Evidence-based conclusions support or refute the hypothesis and further research suggested
Methodology a system of methods used in a particular area of study or activity	Respond to a provocation by wondering, questioning, identifying, & defining	Identify a challenge Define the problem	Define the issue Ask a driving question	Empathise Empathise to scope problem Create the design brief	Look, listen & learn Ask lots of questions	Define	Tuning in	Engage	Ask a question Identify an issue
N.B. the stages of learning sequenced are not always linear. There are iterative cycles of reviewing and refining understanding to better achieve the final outcomes	Research	Background research Outline critical specifications	Research	Define Research for inspiration, investigation and analysis	Understand the process or problem	Discover	Finding out	Explore	Background research
	Imagine Plan	Brainstorm, evaluate and choose a solution	Plan Design and brainstorm	Ideate Generate ideas and develop concepts	Navigate ideas	Dream	Sorting out	Explain	Pose hypothesis Develop & test protocols
	Create	Develop prototype and iterate a test cycle	Create	Prototype & Test Test against design brief parameters	Create a prototype	Design	Going further	Elaborate	Experiment Employ fair test process
	Asses & improve	Improvement for final product	Critique and Revise	Assess Modify & refine to meet brief	Highlight & fix	Deliver	Making connections	Evaluate	Analyse data Make conclusions
	Communicate & share	Communicate & celebrate success	Performance Understanding Culminating event	Present to stakeholders	LAUNCH to an audience	Debrief	Taking action	Share	Present conclusions

Figure 1: STEM education methodologies – A comparison of approaches, philosophies and sequences of learning, matrix developed for Melbourne Archdiocese Catholic Schools by Waldon, 2016; modified by Waldon and Chiavaroli, 2020. See Appendix 1 for the references.

PROVOCATIONS, CONTENTIOUS ISSUES AND INITIATING QUESTIONS

To hook students into learning great inquiries, start with strong provocations. Developing a compelling question or problem to be solved can generate the desire and deep-seated need to overcome the unsettling experience of stepping outside the students' comfort zone to identify and study what needs to be learnt, and create an unknown solution.

Harpaz and Lefstein (2005) challenged the traditional models of teaching with a framework they described as a community of thinking, where students created their knowledge and understanding beyond the industrial model of essential knowledge, decided by policy, taught and told by teachers and ingested or learnt by students. The framework is built on constructivist learning theory; a student focused paradigm of learning, based on the psychology of acquisition of knowledge and meaning, where learning is built (constructed) on prior embedded experience. The framework consists of three stages, commencing with fertile questions, stimulating research and a concluding performance of understanding.

Fertile questions

The focus on fertile questions as driving an inquiry is considered an essential component of curriculum innovation, stimulating student engagement and motivation to research and learn. Pedagogical practices which privilege questioning as a learning tool for clarifying, exploring and explaining, recognise the opportunities offered to learners to build meaning and a deeper understanding of content, by involving creative energy and thinking into challenging assumptions and existing knowledge. Fertile questions as described by Harpaz and Lefstein (2005) have the following characteristics:

- **Open** – several different or competing answers (not specifically correct or incorrect).
- **Undermining** – necessitates the learner challenging their basic assumptions.
- **Rich** – not readily 'googleable' answers, requiring careful, detailed research, often leading to further subsidiary questions.
- **Connected** – relevant to the learner.

- **Charged** – has an ethical dimension.
- **Practical** – is able to be researched with available resources and within the parameters of the inquiry.

Reflecting similar understandings of questioning, Murdoch (2015) makes distinctions between the many types of questions based on their purpose, such as eliciting information or answers to stimulating inquiries and engaging curiosity. She defines 'great' questions with which to engross students as those that:
- Can be investigated in multiple ways
- Invite multiple responses and perspectives
- Connect to the world beyond current experience – it matters and is relevant
- Has 'intellectual bite' – being unsettling and thought provoking
- Contains concepts that are transferable to other contexts or situations

The characteristics of fertile questions and their intrinsic motivation for thinking and investigation, can be fashioned by teachers into exciting provocations. Prompts, designed to provoke learning, can be categorised as:
- **Experiential** – excursions and incursions which elicit a challenge or call to action e.g. Zoos Victoria STEM design challenges
    - Community conservation campaigns
    - Designing animal enclosures and enrichment experiences to augment welfare
    - Enhancing visitor experiences for people with varying disabilities
- **Written**
    - Journals, newspapers, research articles, infographics
    - Guiding questions (e.g. 'does justice for all include animals?')
    - Design briefs - a document outlining the deliverables, parameters and scope of a project. Create a solution for … using … (e.g. Apollo 13 'putting a square peg in a round hole CO_2 scrubber', a life or death challenge)
- **Visual**
    - Video (e.g. orangutan asking deaf girl for help in sign language – Figure 2)
    - Stimulus images – Figure 3

Figure 2: Orangutan asks deaf girl for help in sign language (Rainforest action group protesting tropical rainforest destruction to create palm oil plantations https://www.youtube.com/watch?v=G32YehcdUAw)

Exploration of contentious issues challenges students to apply reasoning to an argument and to take a stand and advocate for their chosen side. Usually ethical principles and thinking are activated. Common social issues which are meaningful to the individual and the group include evaluating needs vs wants, and reflecting on social justice and the common good. Empathy and compassion are galvanised and drive actions to solve problems.

There are many issues in our society to which students are extensively exposed through social media that cause anxiety for students with controversial solutions. Problems include impacts of climate change, environment and loss of habitat, sustainable energy solutions, gender equity, food security, inequitable distribution of wealth and the corollary issues of homelessness, disability and disadvantage and access to resources.

Figure 3: Stimulus images of contemporary social and environmental problems compiled from online sources 2020

PROJECT BASED LEARNING

The traditional model of teaching is where the teacher provides the approved content for students to learn, students learn the content and then assessments, tests and challenges are assigned to demonstrate that the content has been successfully learnt.

Within project based learning an initiating event provides the challenge and motivation for learning, the necessary content to accomplish the challenge is identified and learning takes place and is applied in context to complete the project. When assessing projects, seeking out opportunities to elucidate evidence of learning is preferable.

Project based learning (PBL) is defined as *"...a teaching method in which students gain knowledge and skills by working for an extended period of time to investigate and respond to an authentic, engaging and complex question, problem or challenge."* (Buck Institute for Education, n.d.). The philosophy is that by challenging students to engage in real world and personally meaningful projects, they will be motivated to undertake the

learning they need to address whatever issue or challenge that has piqued their interest. Features of PBL include:
- Extended periods of time to enable sustained inquiry
- Hands-on investigation to build conceptual understanding
- Opportunities for thinking critically, creatively and analytically
- A broad range of resources for research and response
- A scaffolded and supported process combining
  - An initiating event stimulating engagement often through provocations or contentious issues
  - Benchmarking activities that include constructive, formative feedback
  - A culminating event or performance of understanding where learning is shared and communicated learning, establishing the mastery of skills and content.

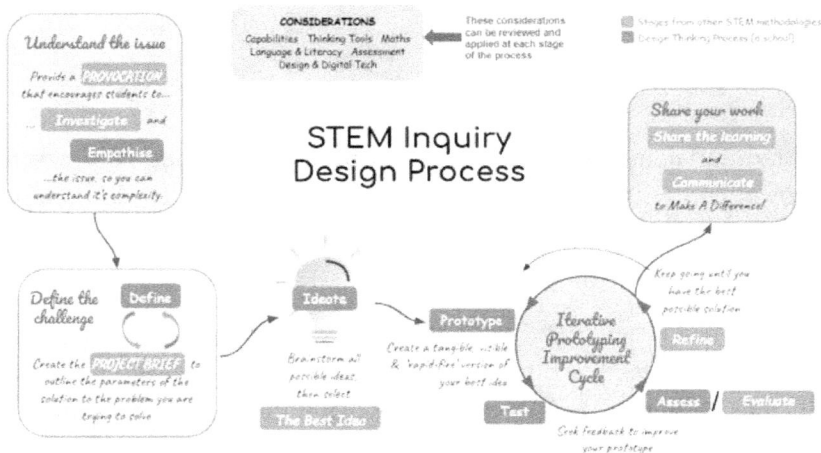

Figure 4: STEM inquiry design process combining design thinking (Stanford d-school) and STEM methodologies, prepared for Melbourne Archdiocese Catholic Schools professional learning by Waldon 2018; modified by Waldon and Chiavaroli 2020

The essential stages of designed STEM inquiry projects are:
- Defining the parameters of the project by understanding the issue or problem.
- An ideation process to persist in teasing out multiple potential solutions before selecting the best one.
- An iterative prototyping cycle of improvement.
- A communication process of sharing to demonstrate understanding.

At each stage there are skills of thinking and capabilities which can be developed and assessed. Considerations of the tools which provide the input needed to achieve the requisite outputs can be planned for, taught and practiced either explicitly prior to the commencement of projects, or incidentally as the needs arise. The logistics of project design are contingent on the specific context of the school culture and the students' next steps in learning.

PEDAGOGICAL PRACTICE FOR LEARNING & TEACHING

> *"Pedagogical expertise enables Catholic educators to shape a local curriculum that will maximise the growth of every learner."*
> Horizons of Hope, Pedagogy Foundation Statement (CEM, 2016)

Deploying pedagogical expertise, teachers can facilitate effective STEM inquiries offering:
- Deep learning that animates learners in authentic and purposeful experiences that are life changing and truth seeking.
- Powerful teaching that builds a culture of learning together to achieve the highest standards possible, underpinned by a strong knowledge of curriculum and effective pedagogies.
- Authentic feedback and ongoing assessment processes that can empower students in their own learning and honours the sacred dignity of each person.

Supporting the constructivist approach to learning children learn best when they are actively engaged in constructing something that has a personal meaning to them, *".. a sand castle or a cake, a Lego house or a corporation, a computer program, a poem, or a theory of the universe"* (Papert, 1993).

Elements of the Pedagogical Content Knowledge (PCK defined by Shulman, 1986) a teacher requires to design and facilitate an effective STEM inquiry project for gifted and talented students combine and incorporate:
- Systems thinking
- Creating mindsets
- Enabling flow
- Strategic questioning

Systems thinking

Dictated by the demands of the curriculum and driven by high stakes testing, the prevalent model of teaching and learning is isolating specific content areas of the curriculum. Particularly in secondary schools, there are significant challenges to moving beyond the discipline silos. These current paradigms of engaging students with subject specific content tend to reinforce students' beliefs in the segregation of knowledge (e.g. Vignette 1 (Part 1) – the story of Lucas who believed he was very poor in mathematics, however when applied in the context of building and launching rockets, demonstrated mathematical understanding and competency several years in advance of his school year level). In any effective enterprise or undertaking, the capacity to transfer prior learning into novel contexts entails the consideration of the ecosystem as a whole.

Systems thinking (originally defined by Professor Forrester, founder of the Systems Dynamic Group at MIT's Sloan School of Management in 1956), is a methodology that considers the interrelationships of all the constituent elements of any system and how the system is maintained by understanding the impact of altering any component of that system and balancing and reinforcing those components. In education, developing students' capacity to reflect on their learning holistically, encourages them to consider prior learning in any area and its potential application in alternative contexts. STEM inquiry projects inherently emphasise the skills of systems thinking to analyse and solve problems and integrate knowledge from across disciplines, providing practice of fundamental elements including project management skills and feedback.

Creating positive growth mindsets

Many gifted students fail to flourish in the senior years of schooling, because they've not learnt how to fail successfully or persist in developing study skills to take them beyond what knowledge is naturally easy for them to acquire. After retraining as a secondary maths teacher, Duckworth observed that unrelated to IQ levels and innate talent, some students did better than others in long-term challenges. In her 2013 TED talk *Grit: the power of passion and perseverance*, she reflected, "Some of the best performers didn't have the highest IQ score, and some of smartest kids weren't doing so well." (Duckworth, 2013). She defined grit as the capacity to consistently sustain effort towards a goal despite struggling, faltering and temporary failure and resilience as the ability to bounce back and continue to pursue that goal in those circumstances.

In all learning a positive mindset is essential to undertake the hard work and struggle of addressing misconceptions and building new understandings. In the contemporary learning environments of continuously evolving technologies, no matter whether its 3D printers, robotics or computer aided design (CAD) programs, a matching skill set is necessary to deploy these resources to their full potential and the right mindset is necessary to persist in developing these skills.

> *"An important restriction of education is that teachers cannot simply transmit knowledge to students, but students need to actively construct knowledge in their own minds. That is, they discover and transform information, check new information against old, and revise rules when they do not longer apply. This constructivist view of learning considers the learner as an active agent in the process of knowledge acquisition"* (Olusegun, 2015).

Carol Dweck confronted one of the oldest debates in psychological theory on 'nature vs nurture', and similarly to Duckworth, noted that giftedness and innate talent didn't guarantee success in life and that learning environments and mindsets were essential contributing factors and that a 'growth' mindset could be fostered through as an approach to learning.

"Individuals who believe their talents can be developed (through hard work, good strategies, and input from others) have a growth mindset. They tend to achieve more than those with a more fixed mindset (those who believe their talents are innate gifts). This is because they worry less about looking smart and they put more energy into learning ... Having a growth mindset involves understanding that taking appropriate risks sometimes leads to failure. The difference, though is in how a person with a growth mindset defines and rebounds from that failure." (Dweck, 2016)

A growth mindset is acquired and improved by:
- Embracing challenges
- Persisting in the face of setbacks
- Understanding that mastery is a result of hard work and effort expended
- Openness to accepting critique to improve understanding
- Being inspired and learning from others

"It is not enough to shift one's mindset. We also need a healthy dose of grit and resilience to achieve short and long-term goals." (Dweck, 2016)

ZPD, flow and the gamification of learning

In his report for the Centre for Strategic Education, Masters encapsulated the critical role of assessment in student learning, *"the one fundamental purpose of assessment in education is to establish and understand where learners are in an aspect of their learning at the time of assessment"* (Masters, 2014). Whilst many gifted students can progress quickly and be accelerated through content areas that match their special aptitudes, they are often not challenged to broaden their skills, frequently resulting in boredom and disengagement. Standard models of summative assessments can certainly pinpoint their academic capacity and advancement in specific curriculum areas, but can't measure engagement or complementary skills, such as the capacity to creatively apply mathematical learning in novel situations. Proficient teachers develop the facility to establish where their gifted students are in all aspects of engagement with their learning and when and how they need to be challenged to move beyond their comfort zone or areas where they have mastery. When engaged in project based learning, goal-setting, benchmarking and formative assessments enable teachers to analyse and distinguish their students' position in the learning cycle, which directs the appropriate next steps in learning.

Students can become disengaged, either if they are insufficiently challenged leading to apathy and boredom, or if they are challenged beyond their perceived capacity to improve and can become anxious. In writing on positive psychology Csikszentmihalyi (1975) first described a flow state as an optimal experience that occurs at the sweet spot of balance between the level of difficulty of the task and the level of skill required to attempt the task. In a state of flow students will be wholly absorbed in the task for extended periods of time. To create tasks that enable flow and continuous engagement, involves building scaffolded experiences, with achievable and progressively more difficult goals, immediate and constructive feedback through the progression and the constant balance of difficulty and skill.

In his seminal work on developmental psychology, Lev Vygotsky defined the zone of proximal development (ZPD) as, *"the distance between the actual developmental level as determined by independent problem solving and the level of potential development as determined through problem-solving under adult guidance, or in collaboration with more capable peers"* (Vygotsky, 1978).

For educators ZPD is the space at which students need support to progress to the next level of their skill development, or understanding, with sufficient challenge for engagement, but without the frustration of too big a step forward, being beyond their learning capacity. It is a fine distinction between the experience of flow in skills practice and ZPD, which requires the extra push or support to move forward. As facilitators of learning, establishing a student's ZPD is a valuable tool in PCK.

Gamification is when gaming strategies are applied in "nongame contexts to enhance experience and modify behaviour." (Lidwell et al., 2015). Gamification encourages ongoing commitment to practice and entails measuring and rewarding preferred behaviours by providing frequent feedback and demonstrating successful achievements (often visually). It also allows the opportunity to fail without criticism and then support the failure with coaching and instructional feedback, to rectify the misunderstanding or yet to be achieved skill.

Gamification of learning has become a popular teaching strategy, based in the psychology of learning, and leveraging engaging activities and intrinsic rewards at appropriate intervals; to maintain motivation, increase attention span, encourage active learning, reduce stress and build a love of learning for its own sake. Papp (2017) researched how teachers can use what the developers of multimedia games have learnt, as a model for supporting students to develop a passion for academic subject areas. When gaming strategies, elements and frameworks were introduced in classes, students were found to have increased motivation and engagement and improved learning, whilst preserving the integrity of learning outcomes. Stimulating this passion to learn is essential for all students and particularly for gifted students, as the capacity to bounce back from failure is an inherent component of game play.

> *"Too often in education we don't want to try something new until we see examples of other schools or teachers who have already done it. Advances in education do not come from imitation; they come from innovation"* (Guskey, 2018)

Strategic questioning

Part of the PCK a teacher requires to facilitate an effective inquiry project is the capacity to use strategic questions at each stage of the project to encourage students to go further and tease out additional learning. Rather than seeking a specific 'correct' answer or solution, students can be empowered by minimal astute interventions, through appropriate hints and introduction of subtle uncertainties.

The story of Carolyn's investigations into bee colony collapse that was a topic of interest to her, and her proposed solution of designing and creating robotic bees is encapsulated in the summary of her learning journey. Her inquiry project successfully engaged her curiosity and commitment to acquiring essential knowledge to problem-solve, throughout her time learning from home during the COVID-19 Melbourne shutdown. She received ongoing critical support from her teachers and school at each stage of her learning journey. Functioning as facilitators to catalyse each successive goal, teachers included nuanced, strategic questioning as part of scaffolded benchmarking and feedback stages of her project. Carolyn submitted this project to the 2020 STEM MAD Student Showcase and her work was recognised with a number of major awards.

STEM MAD is an initiative of Melbourne Archdiocese Catholic Schools. Teams of students are invited to respond to issues of concern to them and take action that matters by designing and creating a service, product or innovation to make a difference (MAD) to help others or the environment. https://sites.google.com/vic.catholic.edu.au/stemmad

> **Vignette 3 – Carolyn and the robotic bees**
>
> Carolyn was a high-achieving student in year 8 at a Catholic secondary college and undertook a STEM project, inspired to create an innovative solution to the global problem of bee colony collapse, with the potential impact of massive loss of pollinators leading to world food scarcity in the future. Carolyn extensively researched reasons for global bee deaths.
>
>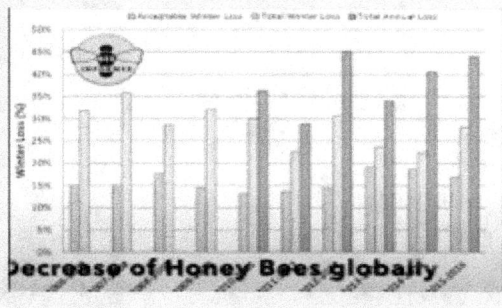

She decided that an effective 'best' solution would be to develop a robotic bee which could act as a pollinator. This was an outstanding example of 'Moonshot Thinking' (a radical or innovative solution to a huge problem, often using disruptive technology). At this stage she had a great idea but wasn't sure where to go next to take it to reality.

Teacher Intervention 1: Carolyn was challenged to create a prototype which could demonstrate the possibility of bringing a robotic bee into existence. By strategic questioning she was encouraged to consider what sensors would be needed for her bees to locate pollen flowers and collect nectar. She was offered a selection of digital tools to help her develop her first prototype, such as BBC Micro:bits or Makey Makey that have extensive capacity to code sensors. She was also offered computer aided design (CAD) programs such as SketchUp and Tinkercad to make 3D models.

Carolyn willingly embraced the opportunity, developing her initial prototype in Tinkercad and testing coding of sensors. She then went beyond what was suggested, sculpting a physical copy of her 3D digital model and considering the type of materials needed to make her robotic bee weatherproof and light enough to fly.

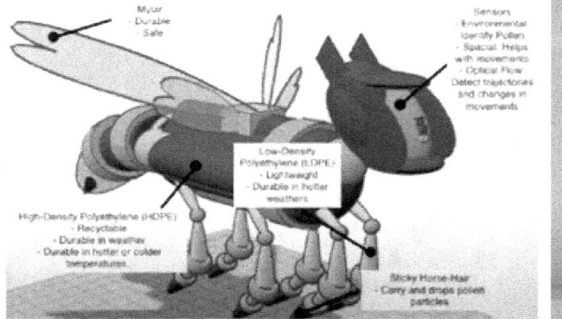 

Teacher intervention 2: Carolyn was questioned about locating and caring for her robotic bees.

After exploring the life of bees she additionally invented solar powered hive chargers, mimicking honeycomb cells with each bee having a unique number plate and matching cell, so that broken, missing and defective bees could be identified and repaired.

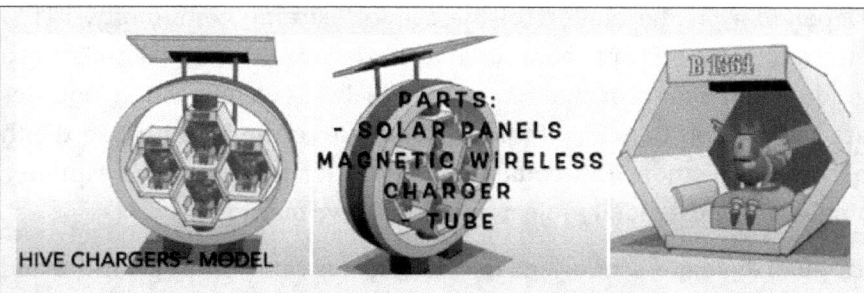

Images taken from Carolyn's winning video entry to STEM MAD goes Digital 2020 Student Showcase for Melbourne Archdiocese Catholic schools.

RESOURCES

Resourcing STEM education is often presumed to exclusively entail access to a range of robotics and digital technologies, however social capital is also essential, developing skilled teachers who can harmoniously incorporate school culture, engaging learning opportunities and environments and TPACK (describes the extension of PCK to include Technological Content Knowledge). In response to the continuously increasing availability of technologies in a digital world, Mishra and Koehler (2006) extended Shulman's PCK to describe a framework for teaching, which incorporates specialised knowledge and skills for effective pedagogical practice in technology-enhanced learning environments.

> "As technology advances, we are challenged to collaborate with schools and lead new pedagogical models for learning and teaching, incorporating new technologies in the classroom and providing new learning spaces to meet the needs of students."
> (Catholic Education Melbourne, 2015)

STEM education can offer opportunities for gifted students to participate in rich, purposeful and challenging learning experiences by engaging with:
- A variety of tools, technologies and learning environments within schools and surrounding communities
- Authentic and reciprocal partnerships between schools and community members, businesses and cultural organisations that have genuine problems to be solved.

Depending on the context of the school learning community, STEM education learning opportunities may be developed and undertaken at a grade, whole school or collective level. Ideally, STEM education inquiries are undertaken in a time frame appropriate to the breadth and depth of the investigation. This could include short, sharp sprints to explore a single skill or extended projects which achieve many goals.

Through dialogue, school leaders and teachers can identify priorities and define strategic directions. Depending on the context of the school and its community, STEM inquiry projects can be undertaken in a number of different models from building specific curriculum elements into discipline based lesson plans to complex project opportunities. Schools often scaffold and move through these opportunities in stages. Examples include:

1. Extension projects, either timetabled into the teaching program or out of school hours, such as:
   - Coding clubs
   - Robotics clubs
   - Maker hubs
   - STEM/STEaM hubs for co-curricular projects
   - Gifted student programs

2. An elective
   - Within one of the major discipline areas
   - An integrated project including and supported by teachers in 2 or more discipline areas

3. Timetabled as part of the school teaching and learning program
   - A shared project with selected discipline specific content being covered in different STEM area lessons within the normal subject-based timetable
   - Collapsed curriculum for 1–2 weeks where students work entirely on selected STEM projects, covering the entire design process from responding to a design brief through the phases to create, test prototypes and communicate delivery of the product or service developed.

- Fully integrated program comprising a lesson being reallocated from each of the STEM discipline areas over a 2-week timetable period and compiled to enable a half day a fortnight STEM extended project time.

Incorporating technologies

Technological change is developing at an exponential pace and the potential of digital technologies for educational purposes is also evolving at a rate and complexity that is increasingly difficult for schools and teachers to accommodate. Advances in technologies such as drones, 3D printing, robotics, artificial intelligence (AI), augmented reality (AR), virtual reality (VR) and computer aided design (CAD) programs, provide ready access to opportunities for technology-enabled innovation, both in pedagogical practice and student learning. New and emerging technologies and online resources are often initially deployed in schools with gifted students providing:

- Engaging and motivating opportunities for extension activities
- Trial programs to test validity of resource allocation for the broader student body
- Potential for differentiating content, particularly for flipped classroom teaching models
- Using adaptive programs to differentiate pace of learning to student needs
- Accessible opportunities for research and prototyping interest-based innovations
- Opportunities for isolated students to connect and interact with academic peers with comparable aptitudes and interests.

The enabling role of technologies are optimised when students are given the opportunities to investigate the extended capacity of tools and resources and move beyond the superficial learning from initial exploration. Facilitating these experiences for gifted students is providing the balance of content that can acquired experientially within exploration, with explicit teaching of concepts and content for successful progression. For example, a spaghetti bridge building challenge is a common and engaging task for middle years' students. In responding to a design brief an aesthetically pleasing bridge can be designed and built in a CAD program such as TinkerCAD or Sketchup, but without an understanding of engineering principles there is no guarantee that the bridge will be structurally sound. Constructing a physical prototype to test connections, angles, strength of shapes and materials is required learning.

> **Vignette 4 – Jonk machines – (Jonathan and Frank years 7–11 from a Catholic co-ed school)**
>
> Jonathan and Frank are two gifted boys in a large co-ed school and had the good fortune to be academic peers with shared interests and have worked collaboratively under the project team name Jonk Machines. With support and encouragement from their design and tech teachers they have worked and learned together on successively more complex STEAM projects, provided through electives, extension and co-curricular activities.
>
> Commencing in the 3D printer club and progressing through code clubs and maker spaces, they worked in an 'Artist in Residence' program, which inspired more extensive projects.
>
> *"... in STEAM you complete something on a project then you realise, I can do this to it, then I can do that to it, then ask yourself, where can I go from here? Well I can add this to it and then add that. You keep adding small amounts. You're not confusing your understanding but you're growing it. You put all the little bits and pieces together into the one main project."*
>
> In 2018 they developed an arcade video game and were challenged to then build the structure to create it as a fully operational arcade machine.
>
> In 2019 using Arduino, coding sensors and lights, they adapted a toddler's ride-in car into an automated remote control vehicle. This integrated project fulfilled curriculum requirements in science, digital and design technologies (coding and electronics), systems engineering and visual communications design (LED lighting and body modifications), demonstrating the potential for co-curricular learning through projects.

Interviewed by their teacher to explore the question, 'Can good Integrated STEM inquiries support self-differentiation for gifted or challenged students?' they favourably compared the integrated learning opportunities in the co-curricular projects to those available in standard single discipline classrooms. They felt able to work to their potential and increase their capacity and skills development.

"... there is more problem-solving and you have to work it out, not receive set instructions from the teacher ... also in the co-curricular you're exploring one issue, but then you'll come across another one that you didn't know anything about, so you have to go and explore that one, it's same process over and over again. Whereas in the classroom it's just, this is your material, do what you have to do, that's it, that's all you're touching, that's all you're doing."

As collaborators they found that they developed further working as a team, where they both complemented each other's skills and also learnt from each other

I've had the privilege of meeting these boys over many years and their engagement with their learning is continuous and their enthusiasm is palpable. Despite being high achievers academically, they continuously go beyond what's necessary. They work out of school hours and constantly challenge themselves to solve problems of increasing complexity.

Reflection: These boys have been fortunate to be in a large school, with sufficient students to find another student with similar interests and capacity. They have also had access to have a range of talented teachers that could both advance them academically, whilst scaffolding learning experiences and projects that developed their capabilities in communication, collaboration, critical thinking and creativity. They have flourished in a well-balanced, supportive learning environment.

APPENDIX I – STEM METHODOLOGIES MATRIX REFERENCES

1. Waldon, S. (2016). STEM Education Briefings and Professional Development. Catholic Education Melbourne
2. Science Buddies (2020). The Engineering Design Process. https://www.sciencebuddies.org/science-fair-projects/engineering-design-process/engineering-design-process-steps
3. Honey, M. A., Pearson, G., & Schweingruber, H. (2014). *STEM Integration in K–12 Education: status, prospects, and an agenda for research.* National Academies Press. https://doi.org/10.17226/18612
4. Markham, T. (2012). *Project Based Learning: Design and Coaching Guide.* Heart IQ Press
5. Hasso Planter Institute of Design (2020). Design Thinking Bootleg — Stanford d.school. https://dschool.stanford.edu/resources/design-thinking-bootleg
6. Spencer, J., & Juliani, A. J. (2016). *Launch: Using Design Thinking to Boost Creativity and Bring Out the Maker in Every Student.* Dave Burgess Consulting, Incorporated
7. Crockett, L.W., & Churches, A. (2016). *Mindful Assessment: The 6 Essential Fluencies of Innovative Learning.* Solution Tree Press
8. Murdoch, K. (2015). *The Power of Inquiry: Teaching and Learning with Curiosity, Creativity and Purpose in the Contemporary Classroom.* Seastar Education
9. Bybee, R. W., & Landes, N. M. (1990). *Science for Life & Living An Elementary School Science Program from Biological Sciences Curriculum Study.* In The *American Biology Teacher* (Vol. 52, Issue 2). http://online.ucpress.edu/abt/article-pdf/52/2/92/44483/4449042.pdf
10. Science Buddies (2020). Steps of the Scientific Method. https://www.sciencebuddies.org/science-fair-projects/science-fair/steps-of-the-scientific-method

CHAPTER REFERENCES

Buck Institute for Education (n.d.). *PBLWorks.* Retrieved from https://www.pblworks.org/

Catholic Education Melbourne (2015). *To Serve and Lead: CEM Strategic Plan 2015-2019.* Melbourne: Catholic Education Melbourne.

Catholic Education Melbourne (2016, September). *Horizons of Hope: Curriculum Foundation Statement.* Retrieved from Catholic Education Victoria Network (CEVN): https://cevn.cecv.catholic.edu.au/Melb/Curriculum/Horizons-of-Hope/Strategy-Statements

Catholic Education Melbourne (2016, September). *Horizons of Hope: Pedagogy Foundation Statement*. Retrieved from Catholic Education Victoria Network: https://cevn.cecv.catholic.edu.au/Melb/Curriculum/Horizons-of-Hope/Strategy-Statements

Csikszentmihalyi, M. (1975). *Beyond Boredom and Anxiety*. Jossey-Bass Publishers

Duckworth, A. (2013, January). *Grit: the power of passion and perseverance*. Retrieved from TED : https://www.youtube.com/watch?v=H14bBuluwB8

Dweck, C. (2007). *Mindset: the New Psychology of Success*. Ballantine Book.

Dweck, C. (2016, January 13). *What Having a "Growth Minset" Actually Means*. Retrieved from Harvard Business Review: https://hbr.org/2016/01/what-having-a-growth-mindset-actually-means

Guskey, T. (2018). Retrieved from Twitter: https://twitter.com/tguskey/status/955527650977701888

Harpaz, Y. (2005). Teaching and Learning in a Community of Thinking. *Journal of Curriculum and Supervision*, Vol 20 No 2, 136–157.

Lidwell, W. H. (2015). *The Pocket Universal Principles of Design*. Beverly, MA: Rockport Publishers Inc.

Masters, G. N. (2014). *Assessment: Getting to the Essence*. Centre for Strategic Education (CSE). Retrieved from Australian Council for Educational Research: https://research.acer.edu.au/ar_misc/18

Mishra, P. A. (2006). Technological pedagogical content knowledge: A framework for teacher knowledge. *Teachers College Record* 108 (6), 1017–1054

Murdoch, K. (2015). *The power of inquiry: teaching and learning with curiosity, creativity and purpose in the contemporary classroom*. Seastar Education

Olusegun, S. (2015). Constructivism Learning Theory: A Paradigm for Teaching and Learning. *IOSR Journal of Research & Methods in Education*, Vol 5(6), 66–70

Papert, S. (1993). *The Children's Machine: rethinking school in the age of the computer*. New York: Basic Books

Papp, T. (2017). Gamification Effects on Motivation and Learning: Application to Primary and College Students. *International Journal for Cross-Disciplinary Subjects in Education*, 8(3), 3193–3201

Shulman, L. (1986). Those Who Understand: Knowledge Growth in Teaching. *Educational Researcher*, Vol.15, No.2, 4–14

Vygotsky, L. S. (1978). *Mind in society: The development of higher psychological processes*. Cambridge, Mass.: Harvard University Press

Watt, H. (2016). Promoting girls' and boys' engagement and particaption in senior secondary STEM fields and occupational aspirations. *ACER Research Conference – Improving STEM Learning: What will it take?* (pp. 34–44). Brisbane: Australian Council for Educational Research

CHAPTER 10

ATTENDING TO THE NEEDS OF THE EMOTIONALLY GIFTED STUDENT

ARRIGO DORISSA

AN INTRODUCTION TO ASHTON

Ashton wasn't similar to his classmates and he knew it. He didn't just think the difference was because schoolwork was easy for him compared the experience of most. He was aware that his thoughts and feelings also stood apart from others his age. Teaching staff knew adjustments to the curriculum were needed to maintain his engagement with the learning and for his emotional wellbeing. The trials and errors that followed proved worthwhile.

In primary school, Ashton taught himself to read and write before anyone else in his grade. He loved novels and films, specifically science fiction stories and their cinematic adaptations. By the time he'd reached grade 6, Ashon was the president of the school's science fiction book and movie club. Meetings were held each week during a lunch break and one afternoon after school. With Ashton presiding over the agenda, the small collective discussed and reviewed their latest discoveries in literature or on the screen. Teachers noticed his ability to successfully run the sessions. How he allowed everyone in the group a chance to contribute and closed down situations when participants went off-topic. He was recognised as masterful with interpersonal dynamics through his inclusiveness and management of the diverse bunch of multi-age and level students attracted to the interest group.

His teachers noted that in social situations, Ashton had an ability to interact with students his age more like an adult rather than a peer. That is, he was observed to mediate conflicts, encourage healthy friendships and diffuse oppositional behaviours among classmates in the school ground. Most notable was his natural ability to sustain appropriate adult conversations. He often conversed with teachers on subject matters beyond the curriculum that often referred to current affairs in the news. Ashton wasn't regarded by his school community as precocious. His teachers nick-named him, 'the old man in a child's body.'

ASHTON'S TRANSITION TO YEAR 7

The start of a new school year and excitement of year 7, was countered by grief and loss, namely the company of some like-minded friends and stimulation his former school provided through a differentiated curriculum and extra-curricular activities. Each day, he robotically followed instructions, moved from each subject from one classroom to the next and silently attended to the so-called challenges posed to him in literacy and numeracy.

The transition from his primary school setting was technically seamless. Academic competence was evident throughout achievement data from Ashton's former school data. The documentation was passed onto leadership at his secondary setting, as was the report of a recent cognitive assessment that revealed his abilities were consistently above average; most falling within superior classifications. However, as evident in his primary school cohort, it was Ashton's maturity that made him stand out amongst the new school community as much, if not more than his academic achievements. Towards the end of first term in year 7, he divided time during recess and lunch between the sanctuary of the library or by accompanying one of the teachers on yard supervision where he engaged in adult, appropriate conversations. Ashton's parents became aware of an unprecedented matter in their son's attitude regarding school; an increased reluctance to attend. The few friends with whom he bonded the closest during his primary education were enrolled in other settings. Ashton disclosed to his parents that school work across his range of subjects was boring and too easy; a situation that added further to an experience of disengagement.

Ashton's presentation on sustainable agricultural techniques caused peers to ridicule him. It wasn't the content of the assignment but the manner in which he sophisticatedly articulated responses when prompted to answer questions by students and teachers. Peer relations were already precarious. He was aware of the laughter from classmates directed at him. Sometimes jeers were accompanied by derogatory remarks. Fueling an annoyance with his new school was Ashton's sense of injustice. He became red faced and occasionally physically trembled with anger when some teachers ignored, or allowed, the verbal harassment he received to pass and without admonishment of those responsible.

Of particular concern was Ashton's social pullback and protest about daily attendance. His parents approached the year-level coordinator and addressed their concerns with his subject teachers; all of whom were receptive. Second term offered Ashton an opportunity to be further challenged with academic tasks. Academic work was something that could be differentiated, made more interesting and richer than standard age and year-level expectations. After all, the group of year 7 subject teachers had already been adjusting their delivery of the curriculum for students with learning challenges and developmental delays.

Competency with classroom achievement was only one part of intervention for Ashton's wellbeing. The struggle to intellectually connect with peers through discussion, mutual interests or on a creative level was what distressed him most. Self-isolation became a sign of how the issue manifested. Ashton was often seen without company during recess and lunch. When the teachers on supervision duty instructed him to play with peers, he appeared disinterested. He'd tried and failed. And, Ashton wasn't used to an experience of failure. Ashton hadn't encountered a sense of disconnect with a school's social environment since his early years, before certain teachers in grade 1 started to understand his abilities and emotional needs.

ASHTON AND THE PRINCIPAL

At some point, every school principal encounters (or will encounter) a student who needs more than what a typical, age-appropriate learning environment offered. In primary and secondary settings decisions to accelerate students remains one of the more difficult and controversial questions that faces educators and parents. Skipping a year level in order for a student to remain engaged with a learning environment based on academic achievement is sometimes the chelf rationale for acceleration. In Ashton's case, his principal developed an insight that above average achievement data was not necessarily the singular reason for acceleration as an option. While many school leaders argue that gifted and talented children need a curriculum that matched them with abilities, potential, and current performance levels; the realm of emotional requirements were often, (1) left unconsidered, or (2) regarded as attended just through adjustments to the curriculum.

Ashton's principal and the school's leadership team observed and noted his presentation. Anecdotal notes were recorded on his verbal communication style, competency with inference when contributing discussion on literature and classroom debates. Leadership invited Ashton's parents to provide background on their son's history of social awareness and emotional intuition and knowledge. The case study illuminated the matter of how a student's mental age also required catering and adjustment to optimise wellbeing. That is, the potential conundrum of 11-year-old Ashton. Specifically, how was a young person with the emotional insight and regulation of an individual closer to 18 years of age, expected to seamlessly gel with classmates; the majority of whom presented as developmentally matched between chronological age and mental age. It was a typical mainstream school after all and teachers of Ashston's year level taught around the emotional abilities of 11- to 12-year-olds.

One of the teachers from Ashton's secondary school was appointed to a leadership position as a learning consultant, responsible for the wellbeing and adjustments to curriculum for gifted and talented students. Her personal interest and professional learning on the matter led her to understand that, unless facilitated, emotionally gifted students were often left to seek their own perception of an engaging with the curriculum. That is, they accepted it was the norm to be bored; an experience that resulted in a resentment, underachievement or disengagement. Gifted students manoeuvred around the emotional presentation of similarly aged peers. Professional reading further informed her that those students sometimes demonstrated leadership and creativity, developed firm beliefs on identity formation (inclusive of cases in which gender nonconformity presented as a factor), they learned how to respond and conform to rules or expectations that did not necessarily made sense to their minds.

The learning consultant discussed with her team a framework for incorporating emotional factors. She proposed that adjustments to the learning environment of gifted and talented students presented a strong argument, both ethically and for humanitarian reasons. It was timely to rethink of an approach to the issue of emotional wellbeing, inclusive of the whole student and not just the parts, such as how they academically performed.

ENGAGING ASHTON

The learning consultant and her team met regularly and the following proposals were drafted:

A framework for a more inclusive learning environment that catered to gifted students was a binary model and described as:
1. Engagement with learning (academic stimulus) and
2. Engagement with others (peers and teachers/emotional wellbeing).

Under the heading of, *Factors for Engagement with Learning (academic stimulus)*, the team came up with the following points:
a. Provision of an adequate amount of academic work that challenged and engaged
b. Opportunities that allowed for learning around the curriculum and that fostered existing talents and explore emerging talents
c. Teachers who differentiated work to meet the student's ability and used language that met the student's lexicon and communication style
d. Teachers who understood the difference between ability and achievement
e. Opportunities that offered engagement with curriculum content and fostered autonomous and self-directed learning.

The team then considered the issue of wellbeing of an emotionally gifted student. Under the title, *Factors for Engagement with Others (peers and teachers/emotional wellbeing)*, they listed:
a. Opportunities that enabled the student's engagement with peers who similarly related to imaginative and creative play
b. A learning environment in which verbal communication was expressed with a similarly advanced lexicon
c. Activities and discussions that conceptually viewed and reflected the world through a similar lens
d. Teachers who fostered inclusiveness, diversity and leadership
e. Teachers who successfully navigated issues of ethics, gender and cultural diversity within the community.

In planning the binary model that catered to academic and emotional wellbeing for gifted students, common sense suggested educators first looked at existing resources within their school. The learning consultant suggested starting with two evaluative questions for her leadership team's consideration:
1. How did teachers currently deliver a differentiated curriculum and how did they offer extra-curricular activities?
2. What physical resources existed with regard to technology, the arts or sport?

Once an internal audit was completed, a question of budget remained. Were there existing finances that provided additional resources for equipment in order to make some of the adjustments for Ashton and other gifted students? There was knowledge pre-existing and shared knowledge of the first part of the binary model that the leadership team developed. Academics and researchers were referred to and quoted (Camilleri, 2018; Munro, 2020; Sousa & Tomlinson, 2018; Tomlinson, 2021). It was a given for the team that ample resources existed with regard to classroom-centred intervention and adjustments to the curriculum to better serve students like Ashton. The second part of the binary model (*Factors for Engagement with Others*) that focused on emotional wellbeing, was lesser-known territory for the team. The learning consultant subsequently included the year 7 coordinator and school psychologist as part of the working party and the audit of existing school resources took form. Resources were then imagined as opportunities for a student such as Ashton to experience an emotional connection with others.

THREE AUDIT OUTCOMES

Ashton's school had a community garden

The school's garden project was a resource that actively engaged students from all year levels. It was purposely designed for students to learn organisation skills, planning, decision making, exposure to the growth and development of vegetable and non-edible plants and day-to-day maintenance of a garden. Aside from the curriculum-based learning in and around the purpose of the garden space, students from all year levels could meet there twice weekly under supervision. The teacher who initially proposed and undertook the development of the project, promoted a socially oriented working-bee during one lunch break and one afternoon at the end of the school day. In addition to bridging gardening activities with aspects from the science and math subjects, more recently, students included in an art elective used the space to study the technique, history and purpose of botanical art.

The resource was recognised as a potential opportunity for Ashton and gifted students like him to engage in conversations with older and mature students within the context of a social activity. Ashton was encouraged to participate. It was anticipated that exposure to older students with a common interest could potentially provide Ashton with positive interactions, conversation more in keeping with his developmental level and intellectual functioning. After a handful of sessions in which he trialled the activity, Ashton indicated that he was eager to continue. His interest in biology and botanical science led to numerous discussions with senior students in which he didn't feel self-conscious about using a verbal lexicon that came naturally to him. An opportunity to develop Ashton's leadership emerged when he opted to take on the leadership responsibility of incorporating more indigenous plantings throughout the space. His objective for the proposal was based on his wanting to encourage the welfare of more insects and other local fauna.

Over time, Ashton's initiative led to the formation of a small working party, a responsibility that had them autonomously pursue research into, and coordinate, the planting of the newly acquired plants. Sections of the garden assigned to edible plants led to an alternative program. Ashton's idea to donate a portion of the harvest to a local food bank, enabled him, the students and teachers involved in the project to forge positive community connections. Anecdotal data gathered by teaching staff noted how the socially-driven activity had a positive impact on Ashston's mental health. He arrived at school presenting as less stressed and with more confidence. It was more than just a large-scale science lesson for him. Ashton socialised with numerous other students from various year levels who, regardless of intellectual capital, shared a common interest.

Ashton's school had a media centre

Students across all year levels were encouraged to utilise equipment from the media centre. The centre wasn't extravagant in equipment: a few digital camera and recorders, tripods, extendable microphone and a limited number of computers with editing software.

Specifically, the working party's intention was to have students explore themes from required readings in the English and English literature subjects. Being an optional route to demonstrating insight with the books on the reading lists, participation in the workshops was voluntary. It was made clear that attendance was required during one lunch break and another session after school each week for six-weeks. A few students took up the challenge. Ashton was one of them. He registered his interest and discovered that the workshop included some peers in year 7, some middle school students and several seniors who were interested in film making as a tertiary course of study.

One of the learning intentions was to make a short film in the format of an interview with a character from a book, or a re-enactment of a scene that could be presented as live-action or through animation. Like other volunteers, Ashton was firstly encouraged to explore the resources in the centre. Discussion led by the leaning consultant and Head of Media prompted ideas of what could be done such as utilising methods of video, animation, scriptwriting, poetry, and podcasts. It wasn't a surprise to the consultant that Ashton chose to work with senior students on a book from the year 11 curriculum. He was welcomed into the older cohort who were currently studying the book. Students in his group were offered learning options through a variety of creative means. A live-action short film became the group's goal. The intention behind the idea was to offer viewers two scenes; one actual, the other an alternative that depicted one of the story's significant plot-points. Ashton's chose scriptwriting as his role and drafted the alternative scene as an exercise on what may have changed for the characters, implications on their situations and the novel's ending had certain events differently played out. Again, his exposure to like-minded students, albeit older than him and who were interested in media, helped with relationship building within his student community. The entire group of students took interest in Ashton's sophisticated insights of character analysis and ability to put his ideas on paper for them to read as a script. Some feedback from staff who witnessed the process and evolution of the projects considered the efforts as an equal if not a more authentic method of assignment than just writing an essay.

Ashton's school had an orchestra

Ashton was encouraged to join the school orchestra. An orchestra that was previously only open to senior students because their level of talent reflected years of training and discipline. An exception was made for Ashton and it was a bending of longstanding protocol that led to musically gifted and talented students. Ashton had demonstrated in his primary school years an astute understanding of reading a musical score and application to the practical demands of interpretation through to string instruments. It was his choice to learn an instrument and his parents were in a position to initially rent a violin that was swapped for a guitar at Ashton's request. However, Ashton found his musical calling during year 7 when he spotted a modern concert harp laying dormant in one of the musical practice rooms. Not the most popular of instruments, in part due to its size and somewhat impractical mobility from home to school, the instrument had been a donation from a well-meaning retired music teacher. Ashton leapt at the chance to bring life back into the harp. Tuition was offered and subsidised through the school's music budget.

For Ashton and other musical gifted and talented students, the school's orchestra provided an opportunity to develop peer relationships and/or social skills through participation in a coherent team with a common goal. Playing music was a joy for Ashton. His practice of the instrument and eventual participation in the orchestra furthered his fine motor skills and coordination to manipulate the number of individual strings running at an angle to its soundboard. Additionally, his intellectual skills were fostered through the ongoing process of reading music and exposure to a gradual introduction of more challenging compositions.

CONCLUSION

Ashton's case study has been deidentified. Names and genders were altered. His parents thought it important that he travelled through his secondary school with similarly aged peers. Appreciating that academic matters could be adjusted accordingly, they worked with teachers to address the importance of his social engagement and emotional connection to his school community. Creativity was required to initially draft what the learning consultant and her colleagues referred to as a binary model. They split the needs of a student like Ashton into two branches that addressed engagement via academia and emotional wellbeing.

In Ashton's case, he required exposure to higher order thinking and socialisation that many of his immediate classmates could not provide for little reason other than they were developmentally typical for their chronological age. A sense of humour, perception of events, development of ideas and verbal expression that Ashton demonstrated, provided clues that he was cognitively different to the majority of students in year 7. His predominantly earnest disposition (further notable by a distinct lack of preconsciousness) cemented the consultant's belief that Ashton's learning environment needed to be more diverse in the provision of social and emotional engagement. Ashton and his family were fortunate that the school in which he was enrolled had some resources, flexibility with timetable and staff to address these matters. What was implemented through learning activities regarding environment, media and music benefited many more students than just Ashton. Although the specific aim in Ashton's case was to expose him to a more emotionally mature student population, the initiatives provided a richer curriculum and social environment for all learners.

Reflecting on the impact of their binary model for gifted students, the learning consultant's working party recognised that the benefits for the entire school community far outweighed the costs. They cited nine potential risk factors that may present if the binary model's framework was insufficient or absent:

1. School refusal due to indifference from to boredom with the curriculum
2. Minimised interest in the curriculum due to a lack of challenge from the content
3. Dislike of peers due to not being educated in understanding group process and not being introduced to activities through multi-age learning opportunities
4. Potential bullying
5. Potential academic underachievement,
6. An emergence of mental health issues that may present as anxiety or depression,
7. Social isolation
8. Behavioural concerns such as attention seeking through inappropriate behaviours due to boredom with the curriculum or peers
9. School refusal.

Emotional wellbeing of gifted and talented students continued to be recognised as a psychoeducational issue by the working party and leadership team at Ashton's school. It took hard work and creative thinking by many teachers. What they achieved for their students was seldom planned and cultivated within mainstream educational practices and settings. As advocates of gifted and talented students, these matters remained of significant importance long after Ashton graduated into middle and senior year levels. The binary model continued to shift and was tailored to student cohorts and at times, individual student needs. The concept of differentiation as something that was limited to an academic process in the classroom became a thing of the past. Rather, a wider lens that included emotional factors took differentiation out of the classroom and into a forum that catered across year levels, inclusive of all students. Parental feedback to the school's principal has been positive. In a couple of cases when feedback was requested, parents referred to the school's practices as a representation of harm or risk minimisation. Although the subject of a healthy social and emotional culture within a school was relevant to each enrolled student, the emotional needs of the gifted had often gone under the radar; at least at Ashton's secondary school. With a foundation of keen interest regarding the needs specific to gifted students, the learning consultant and her team established a learning environment that encompassed a broader educational paradigm; namely, a curriculum that also included adjustments and cognisance for emotional wellbeing and psycho-social development.

CHAPTER REFERENCES

Camilleri, D. (2018, March). *At Risk of Disengagement*. In S. Nikakis (Chair), Gifted Twilight Sessions. Conference conducted at Xavier College, Melbourne

Munro, J. (Speaker) (2020). The Research Files Episode 56: John Munro on gifted education [Audio podcast]. *Teacher Magazine*, ACER. https://soundcloud.com/teacher-acer

Sousa, D.A. & Tomlinson, C.A. (2018). *Differentiation and the Brain: How neuroscience support the learner-friendly classroom.* (2nd Ed.). Melbourne: Hawker Brownlow Education

Tomlinson, C.A. (2021). *So Each May Soar: The principles and practices of learner-centred classrooms.* Alexandra, Virginia: ASCD

CHAPTER II

STUDENT VOICE AND COMMENTS FROM STUDENTS

SUSAN NIKAKIS

STUDENT VOICE

Student voice acknowledges that students have unique perspectives on learning, teaching, and schooling, and should have the opportunity to actively shape their own education.

Student voice involves students actively participating in their schools, communities and the education system, contributing to decision making processes and collectively influencing outcomes by putting forward their views, concerns and ideas.

Although the idea of student agency seems bound up with future-focused learning and innovative learning environments, it is not new. Dewey (1916) for instance, describes learners ideally as agents involved in determining their own outcomes. (It sounds like student voice is closely related to agency!) Agency is particularly relevant within gifted education, with concepts of self-direction and autonomy inherent in frequently espoused goals and curricula of gifted education (for example, Treffinger, 1975).

Agency can be considered as a concept closely related to that of motivation, which has long been associated with gifted students and is identified as a key factor in a range of conceptions of giftedness. Renzulli's (1998) three-ring conception of giftedness identifies task commitment, or motivation, as essential for the demonstration of 'gifted behaviour'. Gagné's differentiated model of giftedness and talent (2012) holds that gifts (natural abilities) can be transformed into talents (exceptional achievements) through a process that is moderated by personal and environmental influences, including motivation. Gifted students who are motivated will have their own voice in relation to their learning. They have agency in their learning. *Differentiation of the curriculum gives students agency over their own learning.*

COMMENTS FROM STUDENTS

So, while you have heard from a diverse number of expert teachers about differentiation let's hear what students have to say about differentiation from their perspective. *No editing has been used on the students work nor how they identified themselves.*

Firstly some year 8 boys:

"In science and maths classes our teachers frequently provide work on the current unit that is one or two years ahead to enable us to take our skills a step further."

"In English we get the same question or task as everyone else, but it is very general and open so we can take our answers or responses as far as we want to. We can add as much depth in our responses as we can and the teachers appreciate this."

"In science we do a lot of theory and practical work with experiments, but my teacher also asks me additional questions that are more difficult. They really test my knowledge of theory and pracs, and the questions require me to apply what I know to provide a great response."

"In some subjects, and extension particularly, we do a lot of small group problem solving and collaboration. We are left to work with our groups for 20 to 30 minutes. We have to think about issues critically and we explore our solutions and responses in innovative ways. At the end we try to present back creatively."

Authors comment: decent differentiation except for the additional work instead of more challenging tasks.

From a year 10 girl:

"Throughout my school life, I have experienced two forms of differentiation in the classroom. Both were greatly beneficial to my learning, as each catered to a different element of my learning style.

In middle school, I found myself with a large capacity for extension. During this time, differentiation came in the form of various options for assessment tasks. The 'matrix' was a grid that presented tasks catering to unique talents and interests, as determined by Gardiner's multiple intelligences. It paired these with the different levels of learning in Bloom's taxonomy. Students were allowed to choose what suited them best, whether that be a musical performance or a video presentation. In accordance with my strengths at the time, I chose to work on a pair of extended essays. To this day, they are some of my best work. Not only did this form of differentiation lead to brilliant outcomes for me, but the entire class also produced work that was of high quality and showed off their unique capabilities.

Just this year came my second experience with differentiation. In the second semester, the course of action is to split the year 10 maths class into two groups. The accelerated '10A' course is designed to prepare students who intend to take VCE maths methods by covering concepts in advance. As a result, concepts are taught and assessed much more quickly than in a regular class.

One of the main things that gifted students find issue with is learning at a faster pace than is offered by their classes; as a result, they experience frustration, boredom, and feeling as though they are wasting time. Compared to regular classes – particularly maths – I've found that the accelerated pace of the 10A class has suited me better. I am able to learn more efficiently and make use of the capacity within me."

Authors note: Ultimately, that sentiment is why I think differentiation is so important. The time and capacity of capable students are being wasted by capping them at the standard of their peers. The fact of the matter is, every student learns differently and has a different capacity to learn. Restricting those with a need for extension is just as damaging as neglecting those in need of assistance.

From a year 7 girl:

"Some teachers will give me extension work in subjects such as maths. For example, in my class, we have groups of students with different difficulty levels of school/homework, but I often find that even this is too generalised. I don't feel like I'm being challenged enough because the work we do in class is what I have learned a long time ago. When I ask my teacher for further extension, and then finish that as well, there's not much left for me to do, because the topic we are learning about can't really be extended much further. I suppose in some cases, I feel that my learning needs can't quite be catered for.

This said, self-advocacy from students like myself is extremely important so that teachers can at least get an idea of my understanding of classwork and whether I am being challenged enough or not. However, many students may find it difficult to approach teachers and inform them of their situation. This is exactly why schools should encourage communication and self-advocacy between students and teachers so that no students are being held back from their untapped potential just because of a simple communication barrier."

Author's note: Untapped potential is a very astute observation from this student.

A year 8 male student who had out of school tutoring:

"When I first started going to my tutoring centre, I had to take a pre-assessment which would determine what level or difficulty of work I would receive. I was put into a course that challenged my knowledge of core subjects and allowed me to grow in the areas I was uncertain of. This does occur in school, but the results aren't as drastic or noticeable because what we learn is the standard for my year level across the country; so if I'm learning at a much higher level of a certain subject, what we're learning at school is still too easy for me overall, seeing as I've thoroughly learned the topic of discussion way back."

Author's note: A good reason for writing this book.

A year 11 male student:

"Referring to Vygotsky's zone of proximal development diagram, I feel that in most subjects at school I am in the centre (student can do on their own). I would like to be given extension work that puts me in the middle ring, the zone of proximal development. This would allow me to further develop my knowledge or understanding of a certain area of a subject whilst still ensuring that I have completely understood the set coursework. As for how a teacher could understand where I sit in terms of my learning and how they could target my learning so that I am challenged, apart from direct communication between teacher and student, I'm simply unsure of a solution or strategy that could identify individual students' learning needs and how teachers could target them. I believe that this is an issue that deserves more attention and should be pondered on more so that students are able to make use of their time at school and actually learn at a level that suits their needs and genuinely gets them thinking."

Authors note: Imagine understanding Vygotsky's zone of proximal development diagram at this age! See Chapter One.

A year 9 female student:

"Throughout my schooling a common theme presented itself in relation to my access to challenging and fulfilling school work. I found that most teachers did not cater for my learning needs as a gifted student. I was not stretched out of my comfort zone and taught new content, I was treated like everyone else in class and learnt to conform to the perspective that simply learning and functioning at the average level of the curriculum was the best for my education.

I often had many setbacks in my learning as school work was often repetitious. I found that most of my teachers did not invest in helping me foster my love of learning; therefore there was no opportunity for learning more within my class setting and expanding myself.

This hurt my morale and put me in a cocoon that did not allow me to experience satisfaction in my schooling performance and individual repertoire of abilities.

Sometimes school can be overwhelming and I know that I don't have to master everything despite misconceptions others may have of me, as a gifted student, just wish to be understood and have someone out there to rally for me. I have an internal thirst to acquire more knowledge and be the best version of myself in all aspects of my life."

CONCLUSION

Authors note: We couldn't put it better ourselves!

CHAPTER REFERENCES

Bruner, J. (1984). Vygotsky's Zone of Proximal Development: The Hidden Agenda. In B. Rogoff, & J. Wertsch (Eds.), Children's Learning in the Zone of Proximal Development: New Directions for Child Development (pp. 93-97). Jossey-Bass. https://doi.org/10.1002/cd.23219842309

Dewey, J. (1916). *Democracy and Education*. The Macmillan Company. Copyright renewed 1944 John Dewey. HTML mark-up copyright 1994 ILT Digital Classics

Gagné, F. (2012). *Building gifts into talents: Brief overview of the DMGT 2.0.* Retrieved from: http://gagnefrancoys.wix.com/dmgt-mddt#!dmgtenglish/cabg

www.ingramcontent.com/pod-product-compliance
Lightning Source LLC
Chambersburg PA
CBHW050355120526
44590CB00015B/1699